100

THINGS TO DO IN
SANTA BARBARA
BEFORE YOU
DIE

To the Gallaghers —

Here's a little something
to help you find your
way to all th...
hot spots! Che...

D0365921

Photo Credit: Tara Jones

100

THINGS TO DO IN
SANTA BARBARA
BEFORE YOU
DIE

● ●

TARA JONES

REEDY PRESS

Library of Congress Control Number: 2015954882

ISBN: 9781681060217

Design by Jill Halpin

Cover Image: Tara Jones

Printed in the United States of America
16 17 18 19 20   5 4 3 2 1

Please note that websites, phone numbers, addresses, and company names are subject to change or cancellation. We did our best to relay the most accurate information available, but due to circumstances beyond our control, please do not hold us liable for misinformation. When exploring new destinations, please do your homework before you go.

DEDICATION

For my parents, who always encouraged me to try new things.

CONTENTS

PREFACE

Welcome to Santa Barbara!

Whether you're seeing State Street for the first time or you're a Santa Barbarian looking to try something different, this book is your insider guide to enjoying our sunny city like a true local. You'll find just about any type of experience you're looking for within this list of one hundred handpicked things to do that reflect the true culture and lifestyle of our not-so-sleepy surfer city and its surrounding towns.

I have had the pleasure of experiencing Santa Barbara County both as a first-timer and transplanted local. As a college student I did plenty of the new kid stuff like shopping Paseo Nuevo and hiking the well-marked trails. For the past decade post-college, as an honest to goodness local and travel industry lady boss, I've had the pleasure of discovering a whole new side to Santa Barbara over the years and realized there are so many things to do here that are great for both the out-of-towner and local alike!

Tourists: ditch the brochures and use this book to help you find the best tacos in town, cool places to shop, or the best beaches to tan those cheeks. Locals: throw on your flip-flops and get out there to do all those things you've been saying you'll get around to "someday."

We may be a cute little surfer city, but it was tough coming up with a list limited to only one hundred things to do! I hope you'll enjoy your time here in paradise and consider this your guide to getting off the beaten path, coloring outside the lines of a typical vacation and the perfect solution to filling up those ho-hum weekends.

Cheers, dude!

ACKNOWLEDGMENT

I would like to acknowledge and thank everyone who helped me in my research of the plethora of things there are to do in Santa Barbara County. Without your input and assistance, I might never have been able to come up with such an awesome list!

A great big thank you to the team at Visit Santa Barbara, specifically Jen Trupiano, JessyLynn Perkins, and Jaime Shaw, for putting me in contact with all the right people. To my insiders and long-time resident friends, Andrew Ngai, David Haaf, Magda Barnes, Anna Taylor, and Carlee Trabucco: I could not have gained so much knowledge of the history of Santa Barbara and gotten such an incredible insider's perspective on water sports without your help. Cheryl Crabtree, thanks again for passing this "little" project my way! And of course, a big thank you to all of the business owners, tour guides, and local employees that let me ask a million questions and so graciously opened their doors to me for interviews, tours, and experiences.

A special thank you to my friend, Lara Cooper, for your incredible talent as a writer and for guiding me through my first book project.

Photo Credit: Tara Jones

FOOD AND DRINK

DO A TACO CRAWL
ON MILPAS STREET

Mexican food lovers, rejoice! Milpas Street has no shortage of places to help you slip into a Mexicoma.

La Super-Rica Taqueria is the perfect place to start. A huge menu board will greet you as you enter the quaint taco stand, but keep an eye out for the small board by the register with the current day's specials. The traditional tacos are a stand-by, but if you're lucky enough to be there on the right day order the popular chilaquiles made with in-house chips, smothered in roja sauce, veggies, and guac.

Once your order is up, take a seat in one of the oldest shacks in town that has an old-school surfer vibe in the heart of Milpas Street, just blocks from the Santa Barbara Bowl. And like Julia Child, famed chef and SB local, you'll fall in love with their handmade tortillas and roasted green peppers that are as big as your head. And, by golly, if it was good enough for Julia, it's good enough for us all!

La Super Rica Taqueria, 622 N Milpas St., Santa Barbara

Neighborhood: Eastside Santa Barbara
Kid friendly if your kid is really, really good at waiting in long lines.

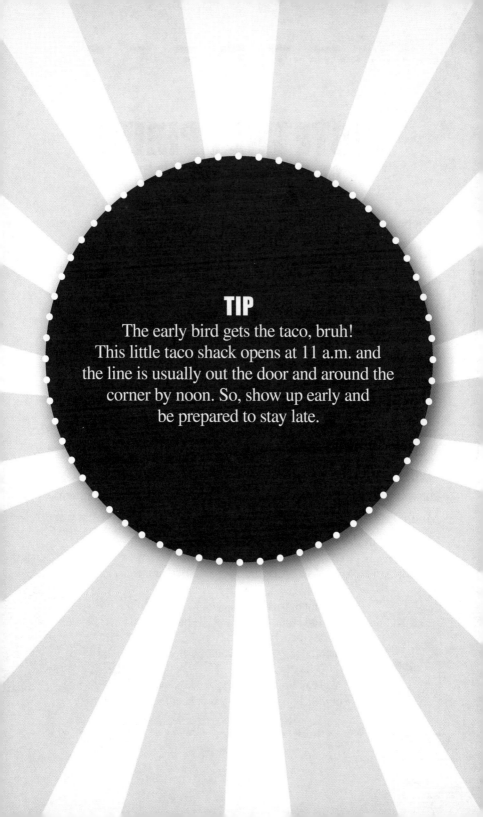

TIP

The early bird gets the taco, bruh!
This little taco shack opens at 11 a.m. and
the line is usually out the door and around the
corner by noon. So, show up early and
be prepared to stay late.

TASTE THE SPIRITS
OF SANTA BARBARA

Celebrate the repeal of Prohibition with a visit to a distillery for sips of vodka, whiskey, or moonshine.

Cutler's Artisan Spirits is Santa Barbara's tiny micro-distillery located in the Funk Zone, but don't be fooled by its size! Inside this itty-bitty tasting room you'll hear all about the Cutler legacy of bootlegging and "bourbon makin'." Throw back extra-mini shots of top-shelf bourbon, vodka, gin, and an apple pie liqueur that is based off Cutler's Grandma Tommy's apple pie recipe.

Or head for the hills to Ascendant Spirits in Buellton's trendy industrial neighborhood for sips of moonshine, vodka, and bourbon. While you're there, take a tour of Santa Barbara County's first legal distillery since Prohibition. And if you're looking for a good beer chaser, wander next door (adjacent to both distilleries) to Figueroa Mountain Brewing Co. for a wide selection of beers, some that were fermented in the leftover bourbon barrels.

Cutler's Artisan Spirits, 137 Anacapa St., Santa Barbara, cutlersartisan.com

Ascendant Spirits Distillery & Tasting Room
37 Industrial Way, Ste. 103, Buellton

Neighborhood: All over Santa Barbara County

You can bring the kiddos and the pup.
But they'll just be having root beer at Fig.

GO ON A
FOOD AND PHOTO TOUR

Get happy snappy on an Eat This, Shoot That! walking tour that includes food tastings and smart phone photography tips. Because there's nothing like discovering a city through your taste buds, amiright?

Join a pro tour guide for the ultimate in foodie discovery of different neighborhoods in Santa Barbara, including the acclaimed Funk Zone that is full of graffiti art, watering holes, and popular eateries. Along the way, you'll get an earful about Santa Barbara history, architecture, and culture plus the story behind each tasting stop. And be sure to bring your smartphone, because food and travel photography tips are all part of the fun.

These guys even do a walking wine tour, which is really the best way to get around once you're knocking back the vino. Visit Santa Barbara's historic Presidio and El Paseo neighborhoods for a few small bites and a whole lot of wine tasting that ends with a delicious wine and chocolate pairing.

Eat This, Shoot That!, eatthisshootthat.com

Neighborhood: Downtown Santa Barbara
Kid friendly if your kid is a foodie and has a 2.5-3 hour attention span.

GET YOUR GRUB ON AT
THE SANTA BARBARA PUBLIC MARKET

If you're looking to do a little self-guided food tour, the Santa Barbara Public Market is just the place to go! Visit stall after stall of local eateries from seafood to pho to pasta to sweet desserts. Kick off your romp around the market with an olive oil tasting at il Fustino, then wander over to Empty Bowl Gourmet Noodle Bar for a rockin' savory and sweet bowl of the Long Tail Boat Noodle.

Next make a pit stop at Wine + Beer for a glass of wine or a cold brew from their exceptional beer list. And if your stomach can take any more, visit Flagstone Pantry for some made-from-scratch, triple-layer veggie polenta that is to die for. If you're ready to go all the way, you have to visit Enjoy Cupcakes for one of their popular blackberry syrah cupcakes or Rori's Artisanal Creamery for their brown sugar banana ice cream made with organic ingredients.

Santa Barbara Public Market, 38 W Victoria St., Santa Barbara
sbpublicmarket.com

Neighborhood: Downtown Santa Barbara
Kid friendly

Other places to visit inside the market:
Culture Counter, Foragers Pantry, Green Star Coffee,
I`a Fish Market & Cafe

TIP

Time flies when you're in the market. So, take advantage of their super-secret underground parking lot located near the rear of the building on Chapala Street to avoid getting a pricey parking ticket. Just be sure to keep your visit to two hours or fewer or you might get cited or towed.

GET AN ORDER
OF ARNE'S FAMOUS AEBLESKIVERS IN SOLVANG

If you find yourself in Solvang's Danish village shopping for wooden shoes, windmill tchotchkes, and cuckoo clocks, be sure to make a pit stop at Solvang Restaurant's walk-up window for Arne's famous aebleskivers (pronounced able-skeevers).

What's an aebleskiver, you say? Picture a lighter, fluffier version of a donut hole served piping hot and smothered in raspberry jam with a light dusting of powdered sugar. While you're waiting in line, take a peek through the window to watch your little plate of heavenly pastry being made to order.

Want to make these forever and ever? They sell specially designed cast-iron pans so you can relive the awesomeness again and again.

Solvang Restaurant, 1672 Copenhagen Dr., Solvang, solvangrestaurant.com

Neighborhood: Solvang
Kid friendly

TIP
You can find aebleskivers at more than one restaurant in Solvang, but don't be fooled by all the cartoonish décor at Arne's. The best ones, hands down, are at Arne's!

GET A KILLER BURRITO
AT A LIQUOR STORE

Some of the best burritos in Santa Barbara County aren't found in the sit-down restaurants, but in the mom-and-pop liquor stores. In the one-horse town of Santa Ynez, you'll find Santa Ynez Burrito nestled inside Rio Market Wine & Spirits that shares a parking lot with the only hardware store in town. Step up to their off-center counter a few aisles away from the front door and have your pick of burritos, tacos, nachos, or chimichangas.

If you're looking for something a little closer to the beach, swing by Tacos To Go inside Beach Liquor in Carpinteria and order up a spicy salsa-laden burrito near the rear of the store. On your way out, hang a left and eat your bomb burrito on the beach like a local. When you're stuffed to the gills, lay back and let that Mexicoma sink in while you nap on the world's safest beach.

Santa Ynez Burrito, 1051 Edison St., Santa Ynez

Tacos To Go, 794 Linden Ave., Carpinteria

Neighborhood: Santa Ynez and Carpinteria
Kid friendly, if your kid doesn't mind waiting outside
and enjoys super-spicy salsas.

ORDER OFF THE SECRET MENU
AT IN-N-OUT

A trip to Santa Barbara isn't complete without making a stop at In-N-Out for one of their California-style burgers. Roll up to the 1950s-style burger joint with the twin palms and join the dozens of tan-skinned, flip-flop clad people waiting in line for a Double-Double cheeseburger with fries and a shake.

If you're looking to stray from the usual, order off the secret menu and ask for a protein-style burger (a lettuce-wrapped burger with no bread), animal-style fries (fries smothered in In-N-Out's secret spread sauce, cheese, and grilled onions), and a Neapolitan shake (strawberry, vanilla, and chocolate mixed together).

In-N-Out, 4865 Calle Real, Santa Barbara, in-n-out.com

Neighborhood: Noleta (North of SB, not quite Goleta)
Kid friendly

TIP
To see the full secret menu, Google "In-N-Out secret menu" as there won't be one posted inside their restaurant and their website only lists the popular orders.

GET A BITE TO EAT
AT AN OLD STAGECOACH STOP

Take a trip off the beaten path and visit a stagecoach stop that has been in operation since 1865. Take a road trip up Highway 154 from Santa Barbara toward the Santa Ynez Valley and keep an eye out for the itty-bitty wood sign that says Cold Spring Tavern. Follow the winding road into the bottom of the canyon and park your car wherever you can along the side of the road.

Once there, walk into the ivy-covered restaurant for breakfast, lunch, or dinner, or stop off for a quick drink at the old saloon. On Saturday or Sunday, enjoy live music and the best BBQ tri-tip sandwiches south of Santa Maria in the great outdoor space among the eclectic mix of motorcycle gangs and Volvo-driving yuppies.

Cold Spring Tavern, 5995 Stagecoach Rd., Santa Barbara
coldspringtavern.com

Neighborhood: Highway 154 near Santa Ynez Valley
Kid friendly

TIP
Most weekends and some holidays, Cold Spring Tavern will host a musical guest (or well-known celeb musician) and not always spread the word. So, it's always worth a random visit on a Friday or Saturday night!

WINE TASTE
IN THE WINE COLLECTION OF EL PASEO

Take an easy stroll through the catacomb-like corner building in the historic Presidio neighborhood for wine tasting from six different wineries and two hidden restaurants. Start out at Jamie Slone Wines, a tasting room that mimics its neighbor, Casa de la Guerra, in style and produces some of the most delicate wines in town. After that, take a short walk around the corner up to Au Bon Climat or Margerum Wine Co. for a taste of some of the best, as these guys are known for being some of the OG's of winemaking in the area.

If you're feeling the hunger pangs, head next door to Margerum's Intermezzo Bar + Café or El Paseo Restaurant, Santa Barbara's only open-air restaurant that once hosted celeb parties during the early 1900s. Once your belly is full, go for round three at Grassini Family Vineyards, MWC32 or Happy Canyon Vineyard.

Take a walking wine tour with Eat This, Shoot That! to get the CliffsNotes version of a full wine tasting experience at all five wineries.

Wine Collection of El Paseo, De la Guerra and Anacapa Sts., Santa Barbara

Neighborhood: Downtown Santa Barbara
Leave the kids, but bring the dog!
Most tasting rooms will have treats for Fido.

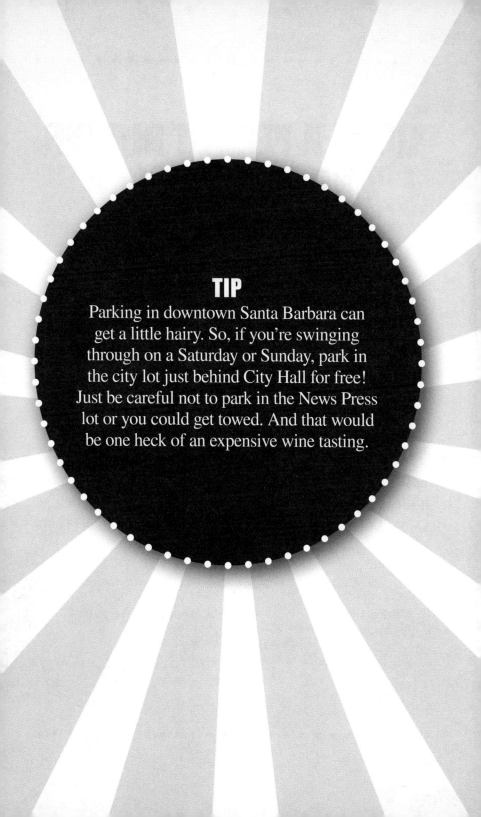

TIP

Parking in downtown Santa Barbara can get a little hairy. So, if you're swinging through on a Saturday or Sunday, park in the city lot just behind City Hall for free! Just be careful not to park in the News Press lot or you could get towed. And that would be one heck of an expensive wine tasting.

GRAB A PEANUT BUTTER AND JELLY BURGER
AT AMERICAN ALE

When you want a good old-fashioned burger, hit up the The Habit's original restaurant on Milpas Street in Santa Barbara (voted America's number one burger). But when you want a burger that strays from the norm, go to American Ale and order the Peanut Butter and Jelly burger.

Sink your teeth into the oddly delicious mix of your favorite childhood sandwich and crispy bacon at American Ale's hipster-designed, sit-down restaurant. If you're looking to OD on bacon try their Make'n Bacon Burger that layers maple bacon jam, bacon, Italian bacon, Canadian bacon, and cheddar cheese into a heart-stopping mix of awesome. After putting in your order, find a seat inside or on their private patio out back and settle in with a cool vintage cocktail, and let the food times roll.

American Ale, 14 E Cota St., Santa Barbara, americanale.net

The Habit, All over Santa Barbara and Goleta, habitburger.com

Neighborhood: Downtown Santa Barbara
Kid friendly

GET THE CUPCAKE OF THE DAY
AT CRUSHCAKES

There are four Crushcakes locations you could visit, but the original is on Anacapa Street in downtown Santa Barbara. Tucked into the rounded corner building, Crushcakes has a standing cupcake menu (red velvet, peace cake, chocolate chocolate) as well as some inventive flavors like margarita and mocha crunch.

After picking up dessert, head up the gangplank and wander into their café for a tasty lunch with an equally silly and unique menu listing. My favorite is the Bappled sandwich with turkey or the Glen CoCo.

Crushcakes, 1315 Anacapa St., Santa Barbara, crushcakes.com

Neighborhood: Downtown Santa Barbara
Kid friendly

TIP
Get a frequent user punch card and on your twelfth visit get a free cupcake or coffee! You'll rack those punches up faster than you think.

GET SUSHI
AT SAKANA OR ARIGATO

A foodie adventure through Santa Barbara isn't complete without a visit to the ever-popular Arigato or Sakana for a feast of sushi and other artful seafood dishes.

If you're hangry you might want to eat a snack first before going to Arigato as they don't take reservations and the wait list can get a little lengthy, especially on the weekends. Once you're seated, put in an order of the "Local's Only" and be impressed when it is delivered to your table while still on fire. When the fire goes out, pick your seafood and vegetable goodies out of the giant shell. If you're still hungry, these guys whip up a mean sushi roll or plate of sashimi.

Take your sushi love up a notch at Sakana in Montecito. The whole menu at this joint is page after page of specialty rolls filled with non-traditional ingredients, like the truffle soy in the Habanero Yellow Tail Melt. And get your camera ready when your plate arrives, as each dish is slathered in different sauces that look like a Jackson Pollock painting.

Arigato, 1225 State St., Santa Barbara, arigatosb.com

Sakana, 1046 Coast Village Rd. #K, Santa Barbara

Neighborhood: Downtown Santa Barbara and Montecito
Kid friendly, if your kid digs raw fish and waiting for seating.

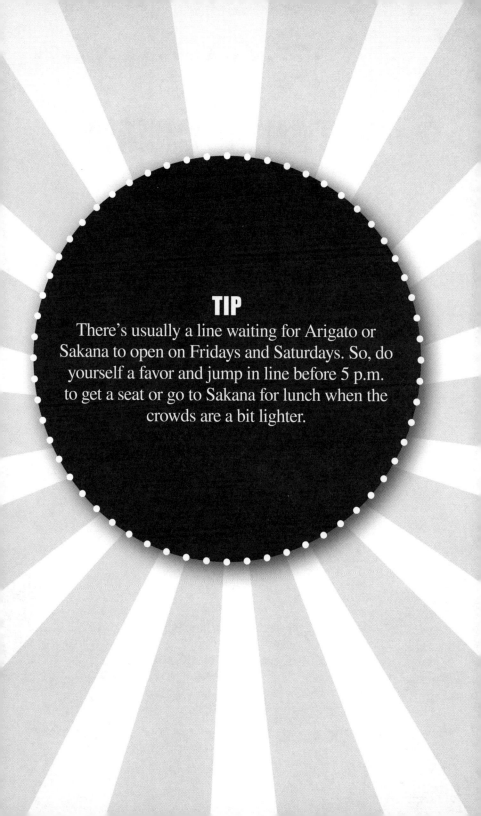

TIP

There's usually a line waiting for Arigato or Sakana to open on Fridays and Saturdays. So, do yourself a favor and jump in line before 5 p.m. to get a seat or go to Sakana for lunch when the crowds are a bit lighter.

GET AN ICE CREAM SANDWICH
AT MCCONNELL'S ICE CREAM

Get a delectable ice cream sandwich from McConnell's Fine Ice Creams, Santa Barbara's favorite ice cream parlor since the 1950s. The original store is on Mission and De La Vina Streets, but my favorite is the one on State Street with their open-air loft with a lot more seating and elbowroom.

Sometimes decisions are hard. So, belly up to the counter to sample over fifteen different flavors from the ice cream case and then choose between several different cookies that are as big as your hand spread wide to bookend that perfectly creamy goodness.

McConnell's Fine Ice Creams, 728 State St., Santa Barbara
mcconnells.com

Neighborhood: Downtown Santa Barbara
Kid friendly

GET A SLICE OF PIE
AT SIMPLY PIES

Don't let the location of this tiny out-of-the-way sweet and savory pie shop keep you from getting a slice of the best pie in town.

Located near the hospital in Goleta, this little place is tucked away a few feet from the street in what looks like an old clapboard house from the '30s. Skip up the stairs of the front porch into the cozy shop and get a slice of quiche followed by a piece of Chocolate-Covered Banana or Lemon Dream pie. Enjoy your order inside the shop or find a spot to plunk down on the front porch.

Simply Pies, 5392 Hollister Ave., Santa Barbara, simplypiessb.com

Neighborhood: Noleta
Kid friendly

TIP
If you're a gluten-free gal like me, you'll enjoy their certified GF options!

GO TO THE
LEMON AND AVOCADO FESTIVALS

Join the hundreds of attendees that swarm Girsch Park in Goleta and Linden Avenue in Carpinteria for the yearly lemon and avocado festivals. Both festivals are free to the public and take place in the early fall; promising tasty treats like lemon meringue pie, lemon beer, and avocado ice cream. Wander your way through the various stands and tables boasting the best of local faire and handmade goods. Before you go home, stock up on all the locally grown citrus and green fruits so you can try your hand at making your own concoctions and recipes.

lemonfestival.com, avofest.com

Kid friendly, leave Fido at home

GET A SURF DOG
ON THE CARPINTERIA BLUFFS

Almost every day, rain or shine, you can find a tiny red stand with a giant hot dog on top near the Carpinteria Bluffs trail. Bill Connell has been serving up hot dogs, soda, and licorice for over twenty years with a smile on his face.

Take the Bailard exit in Carpinteria and park in the dirt lot near the frontage road that sits between the highway and the ocean. Get in line for a delicious beef, pork, or turkey dog and then go for a walk with your dog along the bluffs for classic ocean view seating. Bill serves up lunch and an early dinner most every day noon-5 p.m.

All American Surf Dog, Bailard and Carpinteria Ave., Carpinteria

Neighborhood: Carpinteria
Kid and dog friendly

TIP
Check out Surf Dog's Facebook page to see what's up, Dawg. He usually posts recent updates or off-days when he won't be working due to weather.

TAKE A COOKING CLASS

Cooking is hard. But if you have a great French instructor with years of experience to hold your hand through the process, then it's easy as pie . . . or galette . . . or whatever!

Market Forays with Laurence Hauben is arguably the most fun way to learn how to cook in Santa Barbara. Join her and the rest of the group at the Santa Barbara Harbor at 8 a.m. before going on a shopping expedition through the Farmers' Market and various shops picking up the best and freshest ingredients for your cooking adventure. Next stop, the kitchen, where you'll learn step-by-step instructions on how to prepare, cook, and plate your food. After that, you feast!

Market Forays, marketforays.com

Neighborhood: Downtown Santa Barbara
Kid friendly – Laurence has taught kids as young as five years old!

TIP
Be sure to reserve your space ahead of time as menus and places visited are based on who and how many people will be on the market foray.

HAVE A GLUTEN-FREE LUNCH
AT LILAC PÂTISSERIE

Gluten-free eaters, rejoice! Lilac Pâtisserie has got you covered for breakfast, lunch, or dessert. And to all you snarky foodies out there who love a good gluten joke, get a load of the bakery section and be prepared to eat your words.

After ordering at the walk-up counter, get a seat at one of the outdoor café tables if you can and dine like a Parisian. Otherwise, join the masses inside on the black-and-white tiled floor space for a tasty made-to-order lunch that is sure to please the pickiest of eaters. And since you won't be able escape without wanting all the cakes and goodies behind the glass windows, make sure you walk away with a sweet treat for the road.

Lilac Pâtisserie, 1017 State St., Santa Barbara, lilacpatisserie.com

Neighborhood: Downtown Santa Barbara
Kid friendly

BUY PRODUCE
FROM A ONE-HUNDRED-YEAR-OLD URBAN FARM

Right smack in the middle of Goleta, next door to suburbia and the town's quaint library, is a one-hundred-year-old urban farm that boasts the best tomatoes and strawberries in the city.

Fairview Gardens is just a quick jaunt off Highway 101 and has an impressive spread of fruits and vegetables, both from their farm and surrounding local farms, inside their tiny grocery shack. One of the first certified organic farms in California, this farm is open to the public seven days a week and can be toured anytime you like.

Can't get enough? Join their CSA and get fresh fruit and veg any day of the week. Better yet, apply to live on the farm in one of their six yurts on the property and learn all about organic farming.

Fairview Gardens, 598 N Fairview Ave., Goleta, fairviewgardens.org

Neighborhood: Goleta
Kid friendly

TIP

They also offer weekly summer camps
and after-school programs for kids,
where they plant and harvest snacks, contribute
to farming chores, and create cool stuff.
Your kids bringing home their own
tomatoes is way cooler than bringing home a
colored picture for the hundredth time.

BUY
A LAVENDER LEMONADE

There's nothing better than getting food straight from the ground it grew in. And the lavender-infused lemonade is the real deal at Clairmont Farms in Los Olivos.

If you're out and about in the valley for wine tasting or antique shopping, be sure to stop by Clairmont Farms where visitors are welcome to hang out on the property for a picnic, spend the day painting, or simply wander the farm. When you first come down the dirt driveway, roll down the windows and take a deep breath as the rich sweet scent of lavender hangs in the air. After you park, wander into the tiny shack of a gift shop and let the smell of this European variety of mint engulf your senses. Be sure to buy a lavender lemonade before you head outside and tiptoe through the hearty plants and buzzing bees.

Clairmont Farms, 2480 Roblar Ave., Los Olivos, clairmontfarms.com

Neighborhood: Los Olivos
Kid friendly

VISIT THE HONOR STAND
AT FINLEY FARMS

Who doesn't love a good farmers' market? Fresh fruit, huge bouquets of flowers, and friendly farmers to chat up will always beat a trip to the grocery store. And Santa Barbara County has a market going every day of the week, year round.

But if you find yourself in Santa Ynez, be sure to stop by the honor stand at Finley Farms where a wide array of seasonal, organic vegetables and flowers are for sale. Just after Baseline Avenue, you'll see a wooden sandwich board sign that says "Farmstand Open" and a list of available produce. Every box of fruit and veg is well labeled, plastic bags are available on-site, and the scale doesn't lie. No one mans this stand; you're simply on your honor to get what you need and leave the cash in the rusted-out barrel that sits in front of the stand's entrance.

Finley Farms Organic, 1702 N Refugio Rd., Santa Ynez
finleyfarms.blogspot.com
The stand is open April to November, seven days a week.

Neighborhood: Downtown Santa Barbara
Kid friendly

TIP
Bring exact change as the rusted-out barrel is where the money goes and it doesn't make change.

GO ON A SUNSET
DINNER CRUISE

Saturday night is date night (wink, wink). So, grab your first mate and climb aboard the Double Dolphin at Santa Barbara Sailing and drift away on the open ocean for a couple hours until the sun sets. Choose from an Italian Riviera or Mexican food dinner menu (the menu alternates every other week). Then once you're onboard step up to the bar for a refreshing beverage and go through the buffet line for a delicious dinner that pairs perfectly with being adrift with your best pal by your side.

Seasonal: Memorial Day weekend to Labor Day weekend.

Santa Barbara Sailing, sbsailing.com

Neighborhood: Santa Barbara Harbor
Kid friendly

TIP
Ressies for dinner have to be made by 2 p.m. the day of the cruise. And be sure to bring cash for the no-host bar as drinks are not included in the dinner ticket price.

TAKE A CHEESE
PAIRING CLASS

Everybody say cheese . . . er, C'est Cheese! The tiny little cheese shop in Old Chinatown with the big café is where it's at for all things cheese related. And once a month, year round, they host a super-informative cheese pairing night class that usually includes wine, beer, cider, or even chocolate pairings.

Get your tickets in advance on their website (they usually sell out pretty quickly!) and be sure to show up early to get a good seat as the owners of the shop walk you through each tasting with all the history and processes of each cheese and drink pairing.

C'est Cheese, 825 Santa Barbara St., Santa Barbara, cestcheese.com

Neighborhood: Downtown Santa Barbara
Not so kid friendly as most of the tastings include alcohol.

GRAB A SPECIALTY BEER
AT BREWLAB

There's nothing quite like kicking back with a cold one after a hard day's work. But every now and then you just have to mix it up and brewLAB is the place to do just that. So, what's on tap? Whatever the three outdoorsy owners thought would be fun to make!

This little hole-in-the-wall brewery in Carpinteria's industrial park building chain is consistently inconsistent in that they have an ever-rotating menu of beers. Park in the back lot or on the street and walk into what looks like an office building from the outside. Pick your poison from the huge chalkboard menu on the left, hanging on the wall of the tasting area. From lavender to cardamom to coffee, you'll never be short on choices of new beers to try in this cozy, woodsy tasting room.

brewLab, brewlabcraft.com

Neighborhood: Carpinteria
Dog friendly

DO TEQUILA TASTING
AT PALOMA

The tequila flights at Paloma ain't your average college shots. The owners of the restaurant are known for travelling to Mexico every year and bringing back the best of the best straight from the source. Even though this gem is in a strip mall setting, the food is tried-and-trusted since the owners also own Rudy's in Santa Barbara and Carpinteria, the old taco shops that have been local haunts for decades.

Grab a seat at the bar or ask to be seated in the restaurant. Then get down to business and order a blanco, reposado, or anejo flight of tequilas and be sure to ask the bartender about the history of tequila-making to get a full education.

Paloma, 5764 Calle Real, Goleta, palomagoleta.com

Neighborhood: Goleta
Kid friendly, if you're going for lunch or dinner.

MUSIC AND ENTERTAINMENT

WATCH A MOVIE
OUTSIDE

Bring your blankets, chairs, and snacks for a unique family-friendly movie-watching experience while the laughter of dozens of children fills the air at the end of Stearns Wharf in Santa Barbara or in the middle of Linden Field in Carpinteria.

Looking for a more adult movie-watching experience? Then spread out your all-natural fiber blanket under the stars at the Sunken Gardens with about four thousand of your closest friends and neighbors for a series of flicks that range from film noir classics to movies made in Santa Barbara. (Seriously. The blanket has to be made from natural fibers or they'll confiscate it.)

Stearns Wharf (Santa Barbara West Beach)
219 Stearns Wharf, Santa Barbara

Linden Field (Downtown Carpinteria)
Intersection of 3rd St. and Linden Ave., Carpinteria

Sunken Gardens (Downtown Santa Barbara)
1100 Anacapa St., Santa Barbara, artsandlectures.sa.ucsb.edu

Neighborhood: All over Santa Barbara County
Kid friendly on Stearns Wharf.
And feel free to bring Fido to the Sunken Gardens!

Seasonal: Movies run from July to September.

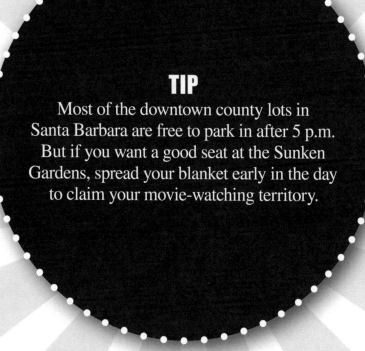

TIP

Most of the downtown county lots in
Santa Barbara are free to park in after 5 p.m.
But if you want a good seat at the Sunken
Gardens, spread your blanket early in the day
to claim your movie-watching territory.

CATCH A DOUBLE FEATURE
AT THE WEST WIND DRIVE-IN

Kick it like it's the 1950s at one of California's last operating drive-in movie theaters. After the sun goes down, load up the car or truck with all the comforts of home, arrive early to stake your claim in the expansive dirt lot, tune your radio to the local station, and enjoy a double feature of the latest movies shown on the biggest outdoor movie screen in town.

In between features, take a minute to stretch your legs over by the snack bar and dive into a cheeseburger or a Nathan's Famous hot dog. And don't forget to get some cotton candy for the kiddies, Daddio.

West Wind, 907 S Kellogg, Goleta, westwinddi.com

Neighborhood: Goleta
Usually kid-friendly flicks, but be sure to check the movie schedule before going.

TIP
Tuesday night is Family Fun Night with a discounted price of $5 per adult (regular price is $7.50 per adult, $1 per kid 5-11 yrs). And kiddos under 5 are always free!

TAKE IN A SHOW
AT GRANADA THEATRE

Don your Sunday best and walk the red carpet at the Granada Theatre. No, really—the whole place is covered in a wall-to-wall plush red carpet. You'll feel like an old-timey theatergoer when you roll up to the valet standing under the marquee.

Once inside, take in the embellished walls, oversized red theater seats, ceiling murals, and chandeliers of this Italian-inspired, gold-toned theater. And if you're looking for a good vantage point of the stage, have no fear! Every seat in the theater has been specially designed to have prime viewing for any attendee and the acoustics are toned to perfection for live theater performances or musical shows.

Granada Theatre, 1214 State St., Santa Barbara, granadasb.org

Neighborhood: Downtown Santa Barbara
Kid friendly is up to you, Mom and Dad.

TIP
Get there early or else you run the risk of missing the first half of the show. Those doors close right on time and the show simply must go on, darling, with or without you!

WATCH A CONCERT
AT THE SANTA BARBARA BOWL

Take in a rockin' good show just about any time of the year at the Santa Barbara Bowl, which is arguably the best concert venue this side of the Mississippi. Do yourself a favor and park on a neighborhood street a few blocks away and walk to the Bowl's entrance. Otherwise, you'll be waiting in the parking line for-ev-er.

Once you're there, hike up the hill to the quaint outdoor concert venue and find your seat, which will probably be close enough to throw your unmentionables on stage. Just about every seat at this forty-five-hundred-person concert venue is a good one to take in a larger-than-life show by the local talent (Katy Perry, Jack Johnson, Crosby, Stills & Nash) and out-of-towners alike.

Seasonal: Concerts run April through October

Santa Barbara Bowl, 1122 N Milpas St., Santa Barbara, sbbowl.com

Neighborhood: Downtown Santa Barbara
Not so kid friendly. Shows usually run until 10 p.m., so you might think about getting a sitter.

TIP
Get your tickets at the Bowl's box office and save $10. Rock on, dude!

ENJOY A FREE CONCERT
IN CHASE PALM PARK

Every summer Santa Barbara is rife with outdoor events, and Concerts in the Park is not to be missed! Every Thursday in July you can enjoy a free concert in Chase Palm Park's mini-amphitheater area across the street from East Beach.

Get there early to spread your blanket and enjoy great local music from big band to salsa. Everyone will have snacks and dinner plates galore, so do yourself a favor and bring a picnic basket with you so that you don't drool all over your neighbors' spread. After dinner, dust off your dancing shoes and join the crowd gathered at the front of the stage to show off your best moves or sit back and enjoy the best people-watching in town.

Chase Palm Park, 323 E Cabrillo Blvd., Santa Barbara
santabarbaraca.gov/concerts

Neighborhood: Santa Barbara Waterfront
Kid friendly and dog friendly, just keep Fido on a leash.

TIP
You'll want to ride your bike to the park if you can since parking is extremely limited on the streets and you'll be walking for at least 10-15 minutes from any parking lot or side street.

CATCH A SHOW
AT THE ARLINGTON THEATRE

This ain't your average movie theater! The Arlington Theatre was built in the 1930s and was designed to mimic a Spanish villa at night. Rumor has it that there are underground tunnels from the old hotel that was once a prominent part of the city that are still in use.

On any given day the Arlington Theatre will be showing a current movie or two on its giant screen. But keep an eye out for the listing on the marquee at the top of the courtyard entrance for appearances of special guest lecturers, authors, musicians, and comedians. Once inside the theater, be sure to look up and notice the starry night sky and balconies that look like they're part of a Spanish villa from yesteryear.

But wait, there's more! Every February the Arlington hosts the Santa Barbara Film Festival that honors multiple celebrity guests.

Arlington Theatre, arlingtontheatre.com

TIP
Special guest nights sell out quickly. So, purchase your tickets online and save yourself hours of waiting in line at the box office.

GO TO A CONCERT
AT SOHO

Catch dinner and a live performance at SOhO and discover new or up-and-coming musicians before they make it big.

Hidden inside Victoria Court, just off State Street, SOhO is tucked away upstairs, secluded from all the shops and restaurants on the street level. Pre-purchase dinner and reserve show tickets to secure an epic seat and a chance to enjoy a local surf or turf dinner. Or take a chance on buying tickets at the door and grab a standing spot near the bar where you can order small-bite plates. If you're looking to do a show on the cheap, check out their performance calendar on the website and score tickets for as low as $10.

No dinner seats left for the show? Grab a table downstairs at Scarlett Begonia for a farm-to-table dining experience before the show.

SOhO Restaurant & Music Club, 1221 State St., Santa Barbara
sohosb.com

Scarlett Begonia, 11 W Victoria St. #10, Santa Barbara
scarlettbegonia.net

Neighborhood: Downtown Santa Barbara
Not so kid friendly

WATCH A PARADE
ON STATE STREET

If there's an excuse to party and throw a parade, you can bet Santa Barbara is on top of it! Every year multiple parades go up and down State Street at almost any time of the year, but the most notable ones to take in are the Summer Solstice, Horse Parade for Old Fiesta Days, and the Holiday Parade.

Summertime is definitely a good reason to hoot and holler! Find a shady spot on lower State Street and take in the creative eclecticness that is the Solstice Parade. Watch as dozens of locals push their handmade floats, made from materials from the Art From Scrap store, up the street while onlookers shake their groove thang and join the final float as it's pushed up to the park in Alameda Plaza. Once summer gets rolling, come back to the main drag to see the largest horse parade in the world, complete with ropers and rancheros!

When the holidays roll around, grab a hot cup of cocoa and a Danish treat from The Andersen's and settle in among the masses to see Santa Barbara's only nighttime parade. Watch as larger-than-life floats and balloons roll and bob down the street and around the forty-foot-tall live Christmas tree that is displayed annually in the center of State Street. If you'd rather catch a parade on water, check out the annual Christmas boat parade in the Santa Barbara Harbor.

The Andersen's Restaurant & Bakery
1106 State St., Santa Barbara, andersenssantabarbara.com

Neighborhood: Downtown Santa Barbara
Kid friendly

TIP

If you show up early enough,
you'll find parking a few blocks away
in the neighborhood side streets and you'll
save yourself from the mass exit chaos at all
the parking garages.

Art From Scrap
302 E Cota, Santa Barbara

Moby Dick Restaurant
220 Stearns Wharf, Santa Barbara

mobydicksb.com
solsticeparade.com
oldspanishdays-fiesta.org
downtownsb.org

SEE A PLAY
AT THE NEW VIC THEATRE

There's nothing quite like a night at the theatre, dahling! And Ensemble Theatre Company knows how to put on a good show with their crew of professional stage actors. Inside the recently renovated, one-hundred-year-old theater that seats about 250 people, all the seats are good seats and the cost for live theater can't be beat with ticket prices starting at $35.

Fancy yourself a theater buff? Check out their special events like the Pre-Show Talk every Wednesday night to discuss the plays before you see them. Or come for Martini Night where every second Friday of the run of a show you can enjoy a complimentary martini and mingle before the show.

Ensemble Theatre Company, 33 W Victoria St., Santa Barbara
ensembletheatre.com

Neighborhood: Downtown Santa Barbara
Kid friendly

TIP
Hey there, twenty-somethings! You can afford to be cultured, too, since tickets to any show for youth under age 29 are only $20.

GO TO THE SYMPHONY

Put your pinky in the air as you enjoy an afternoon of refined picnicking and classical music at the Music Academy of the West.

Join a few hundred people during the summer for a relaxing evening picnic on the lawn, held every Friday at the Academy. Bring your own food and drink and take a seat on the grass or at one of the tables provided. When the picnic is over, make your way around the oceanfront campus to Hahn Hall where you'll enjoy an afternoon of culture and classical music performed by students and local musicians where the performances range from chamber music to competitive performances. And if you just can't get enough of this scene, join them on the weekends for a screening of operas performed live at The Met.

Music Academy of The West, 1070 Fairway Rd., Santa Barbara
musicacademy.org

Neighborhood: Montecito
Kid friendly, if your kid digs classical music.

TIP
Garden picnic tables are available on a first-come, first-served basis. So, if you want to make sure you get a spot, you can put a reservation sign on any picnic table beginning at 10 a.m. the day of the concert.

Photo Credit: Tara Jones

SPORTS AND RECREATION

WALK AMONG THE GIANTS
AT THE SANTA BARBARA
BOTANIC GARDEN

Chat it up with the friendly docent at the entrance booth while getting a lay of the land then, just follow the path around the forty-five-acre property to get an eyeful of the expansive meadow bursting with poppies and lupine.

Make your way around the bend and stop for a sit-down on the stone bench to catch a glimpse of the Channel Islands. After a quick rest, walk down the dirt path toward the forest of Northern California redwood trees and the two-hundred-year-old aqueduct system that used to feed the Old Mission of Santa Barbara's water supply. And if you're visiting on the second Saturday of the month, head on over to the on-site Tea House where a tea ceremony is hosted by a bona fide sensei.

Make a day of it and pack a picnic basket ahead of time—Yogi Bear style--and enjoy your tasty treats at one of two picnic spots on the property that overlook the surrounding flora and fauna.

Santa Barbara Botanic Garden, 1212 Mission Canyon Rd., Santa Barbara
sbbg.org

Neighborhood: Near Santa Barbara Mission
Kid friendly and dog friendly, if you keep Fido on a leash.
Kid leashes are optional.

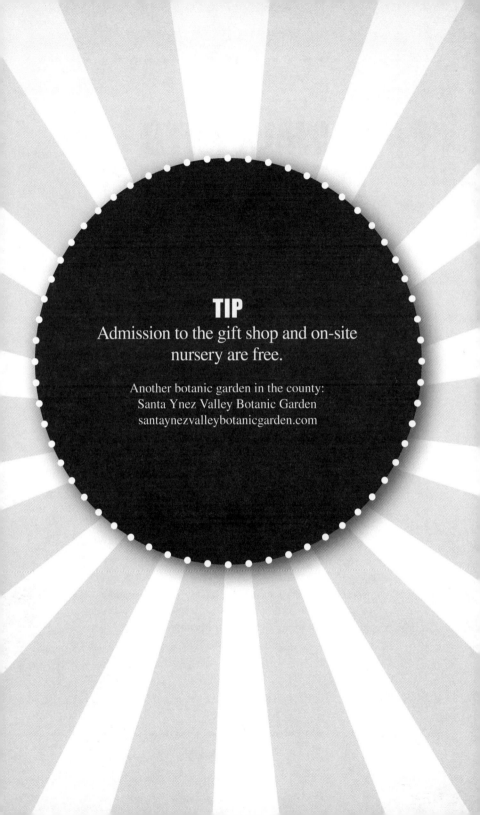

TIP

Admission to the gift shop and on-site nursery are free.

Another botanic garden in the county:
Santa Ynez Valley Botanic Garden
santaynezvalleybotanicgarden.com

WALK WITH
THE BUTTERFLIES
AT THE BUTTERFLY PRESERVE

If you're an early riser, take a walk through the butterfly preserve in Goleta when the sun starts to shine and watch all the butterflies wake up as, one-by-one, they peel off the trees to start their day. Head down the broad path that leads to a forest of eucalyptus trees and take any trailhead since they all lead to the biggest area of the grove. Walk about a half mile and you'll see the tall trees overhead that look like they're holding on to last season's foliage and watch as those brown "leaves" start to open their wings and flutter all around the seemingly secret garden.

After the show, take a short hike up to the bluffs and explore the various open trails that wander all along the plateau, overlooking the ocean. If you're lucky, you'll snag a seat on one of the fallen logs along the trails that edges the bluffs for an epic viewing of the sunrise or sunset.

Sperling Preserve, Goleta, goletabutterflygrove.com

Neighborhood: Ellwood Mesa in Goleta
Kid friendly

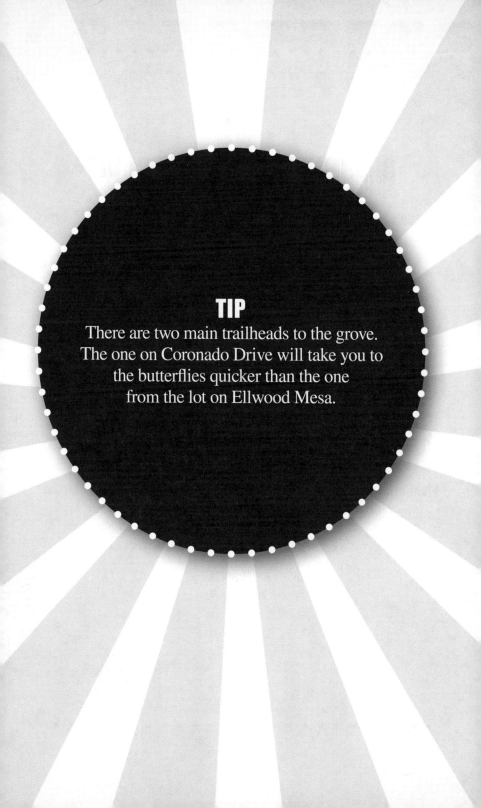

TIP

There are two main trailheads to the grove.
The one on Coronado Drive will take you to
the butterflies quicker than the one
from the lot on Ellwood Mesa.

GO
ON A WHALE WATCHING CRUISE

Practice your whale-calling skills like Dory from Finding Nemo on a whale watching cruise aboard the Condor Express. Bring your camera, a light jacket, and get ready to snap some pics of sea life in action.

Hop onboard the double-decker boat and cruise the channel while the captain steers you alongside pods of dolphins and grey or humpback whales. The California grey whales pass by on both their northern and southern migration. So, you're almost guaranteed to see some tail flips and fin waves!

If you've got questions about aquatic life, ask one of the friendly crew, a Channel Islands Naturalist Corps volunteer, or the rep from the Channel Islands National Marine Sanctuary and National Park aboard the boat to answer just about any marine-related query you could think of.

Condor Express inside Sea Landing, condorexpress.com

Neighborhood: Santa Barbara Harbor
Kid friendly

TIP

If you are prone to motion sickness,
do yourself a favor and drug up hours
before your boat ride. If you forget (like I did),
camp out at the rear of the boat and hold
on tight. At the end of the cruise a crew
member will give you a ginger chew
to help settle your stomach.
And it really does help!

HIT THE BEACH
AND CATCH SOME WAVES

Santa Barbara has some of the most beautiful beaches on the West Coast. If you're looking for a place to get your tan on, hang ten, or go tide pooling, these are the beaches to seek out:

- **Little Rincon (Carpinteria)** – Surfer's haven. This spot doesn't tend to get huge waves, but on a good day you can expect to share the waves with at least ten other surfing locals. You'll need experience, though, to hang ten with this crowd.

- **Carpinteria State (Carpinteria)** – Dubbed the world's safest beach, there is a super-expansive area to spread your blanket and lots of room on the white water for beginner surfers. During the summer months, a little shack opens up near Fourth Beach (northernmost part of the beach) that rents kayaks and stand-up paddleboards. And at low tide there is excellent tide pooling near the south end.

- **Hammonds (Montecito)** – Clean, quiet, secluded. To find this beach, head down the narrow dirt trail that leads to the right just before Miramar Beach's stairs. At the end of the nature trail, cross over the wood bridge and take a left to a perfect, exclusive beach.

- **Butterfly (Montecito)** – Most romantic beach in town, but sometimes the tide is too high to find any dry sand. So, grab a seat on the sea wall (across the street from the beautiful gardens of The Four Seasons Hotel) and watch the sunrise or sunset with your sweetie.

- **East Beach (Santa Barbara)** – Party beach for sure. Perfect spot for beach picnics, tanning, and volleyball. Several volleyball courts are already set up and ready to be claimed for the day.

- **Arroyo Burro (Santa Barbara)** – The dog beach. On the right side is an excellent place to come hang with friends during the day (and sometimes at night for bonfires). On the left side is where dogs and their owners can play fetch to their hearts' content.

- **Thousand Steps (Santa Barbara)** – Cool spot for a short hike. It's fewer than a thousand steps (by quite a lot), but your thighs will beg to differ once you've walked from top to bottom and back up again. And on a good day this little beach gets a nice swell for the surfing crowd and sweet clarity for the divers and snorkelers.

- **Goleta Beach (Goleta)** – The pier on this beach is a great fishing spot, day or night. And the grassy area connected to the beach (complete with playgrounds) is great for BBQ parties and kids. Campus Point butts up against the north end of this beach and boasts a good surf spot for the UCSB students and other local surfers.

- **Ellwood Beach (Goleta)** – Beautiful stretch of beach just north of UCSB/Isla Vista that is perfect for long walks or exploring along the bluffs.

> **TIP**
> Wanna rent a board before becoming a lifer?
> Check out Surf Country in Goleta where you can rent
> surfboards, boogie boards, and wetsuits starting at $10.

TAKE A SWING
AT THE BATTING CAGES

'Ey batter, batter!

Get some practice time in with your baseball swing at East Beach Batting Cages. But before you step up to the plate, get an order of tacos at East Beach Tacos at the gourmet beach-style taco stand that sits at the entrance of the cages. Order the Three Taco deal and get a free batting cage token, good for nineteen pitches. Pull up a chair across from the order window and fuel up before taking a swing at some softball or baseball pitches at whatever speed you're ready for. If you're worried about that taco coma putting your safety in jeopardy, ask the guy at the cages for a helmet before jumping in the cage.

East Beach Batting Cages and East Beach Tacos, 226 S Milpas St.
Santa Barbara, eastbeachbattingcages.com, eastbeachtacos.com

Neighborhood: Eastside Santa Barbara
Kid friendly

TAKE A DANCE LESSON
AT THE CARRILLO REC CENTER

Try something a little different from your usual gym routine and check out a Zumba class, held just about every day of the week, and sweat it out alongside two hundred other dancers in the rec center's old-timey, high ceiling ballroom. Swing an invite from a Zumba buddy and get in for free on a Wednesday night!

Every first and third Friday, after the Zumba exodus, the jitterbug crowd moves in for swing dancing. Show up at 7:30 p.m. for a forty-five-minute beginning swing dance class. Master your new moves for the next thirty minutes while a DJ chooses the tunes. Then, at 8:45 p.m., get ready to really show off what you know as you twirl your way around the dance floor while a live band plays on stage.

Carrillo Recreation Center, 100 E Carrillo St., Santa Barbara
josettetkacik.com

Neighborhood: Downtown Santa Barbara
Kid friendly

TIP
Info on the Rec Center's website about classes and schedules is sketchy at best. To see what other classes the Center offers, stop by their office to pick up a printout of what's available.

COUNTRY WESTERN DANCE
AT MAVERICK SALOON OR CREEK SIDE

If you're coming from the north, head to Maverick Saloon in the little town of Santa Ynez. Roll up to the old west saloon for a late night BBQ bite to eat then head inside the bar, take a quick glance up at the ceiling covered in autographs on dollar bills and bits of paper, and swing a right into the dan ce hall every Friday night for western dance lessons and a night of two-steppin'.

If you're coming from the south, hitch a ride to The Creek Side Inn in Noleta (north of Santa Barbara, not quite Goleta) for a night of country line dancing and two-steppin' like you've seen in the movies. Grab a bite to eat before you get to gettin' at The Bourbon Room next door. Show up early and take the dance lessons beforehand for an extra few bucks. But a word to the wise: some of the line dances are really fast-paced. So, if you've still got a hitch in your giddy-up be prepared to step aside and try to learn from watching the regulars if you can!

Maverick Saloon, 3687 Sagunto St., Santa Ynez, mavericksaloon.org

The Creek Side Inn, 4444 Hollister Ave., Santa Barbara, creeksidesb.com

Neighborhood: Santa Ynez and Noleta
Not kid friendly

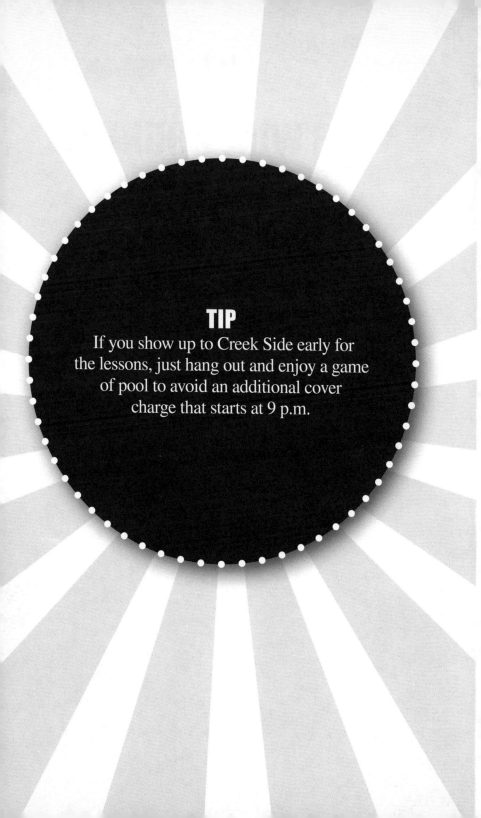

TIP

If you show up to Creek Side early for the lessons, just hang out and enjoy a game of pool to avoid an additional cover charge that starts at 9 p.m.

TOUR WINE COUNTRY
IN A HOT AIR BALLOON

Sure, a drive through the Santa Ynez Valley's wine country is great, but touring it in a hot air balloon is so totally awesome!

Take to the skies with Sky's The Limit Ballooning Adventures for a one-hour ride over the vineyard and ranches of the valley. Show up at the Santa Ynez Airport at the crack of dawn with a cup of coffee and wipe the sleep out of your eyes before boarding your basket. As the balloon starts to rise, hang on and take in the insanely scenic views of the valley, the likes of which you've only seen on postcards.

Follow your early morning hot air balloon ride with a continental breakfast and wine tasting at two wineries in the valley as the friendly staff drives you to and from the airport or your hotel.

Sky's The Limit Ballooning Adventures, santabarbaraballoonrides.com

Neighborhood: Santa Ynez Valley
Kid friendly, ages five and up.

RIDE AROUND TOWN
WITH THE BIKE MOVES GROUP

Every first Thursday of the month a group of fun and crazy locals choose a theme, get dressed up, and ride around town on beach cruisers, road bikes, or anything that rolls on wheels.

Join the group for a free ride that starts at Plaza De Vera Cruz, the small kiddie park near French Press, where you'll see the whole gang dressed to match the current month's theme, like prom or Back to the Future or Monopoly. Start the ride going uptown near the Arlington Theatre where you'll turn around and head down State Street to the end of Stearns Wharf. Get ready to make some noise at all the stoplights, as part of the fun is making a ruckus while obeying all the rules of the road.

Santa Barbara Bike Moves, Plaza De Vera Cruz on East Cota
Santa Barbara, sbbikemoves.com

Neighborhood: Downtown Santa Barbara
Kid friendly

KAYAK OR SUP
AROUND THE HARBOR

Santa Barbara Harbor is one of the best spots for easily getting in and out of the ocean waves. And kayaking or stand up paddleboarding is where it's at if you want to do it on the cheap.

Head down to SEA Landing in the harbor and rent a kayak or stand up paddleboard for three hours for only $15. The SEA Landing office is right on the water and jumping in after you sign all the paperwork is easy-peasy. Start out paddling your way through all the parked sailboats then take a right around the sea wall toward the nearest green buoy that is usually covered with sea lions. On a calm day, you should be able to paddle around in the ocean without too much pull from the current.

If you're looking to do a little more than a basic kayaking trip in the harbor, check out Santa Barbara Adventure Company's kayaking trips to the Channel Islands.

SEA Landing, sealanding.net

Santa Barbara Adventure Company, 32 E Haley, Santa Barbara
sbadventureco.com

Santa Barbara Sailing, sbsail.com

Neighborhood: Santa Barbara Harbor
Kid and dog friendly

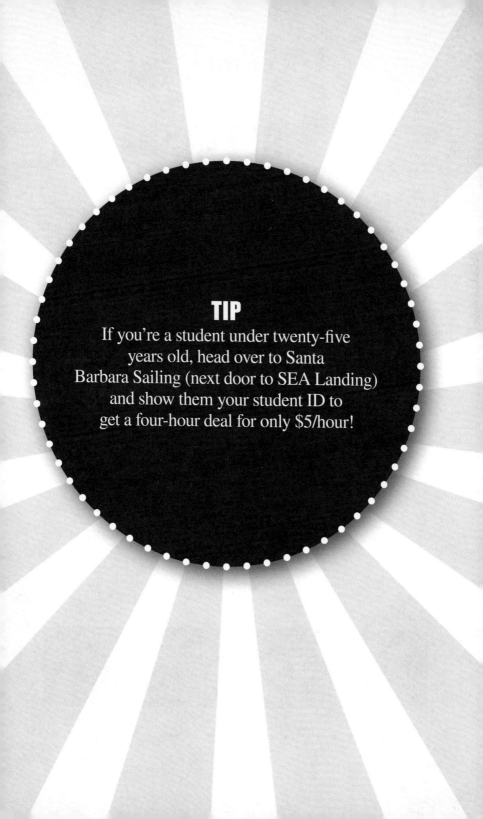

TIP

If you're a student under twenty-five years old, head over to Santa Barbara Sailing (next door to SEA Landing) and show them your student ID to get a four-hour deal for only $5/hour!

GET IN
A ROUND OF GOLF

Keep your eye on the birdie at oak-studded and ocean view golf courses in SB County. Here are a few places to get in nine or eighteen holes of golf.

Hidden Oaks – Santa Barbara
La Cumbre Country Club – Santa Barbara
Santa Barbara Golf Club – Santa Barbara
Sandpiper – Goleta
Montecito Country Club – Montecito
Twin Lakes Golf Course – Goleta
Valley Club of Montecito – Montecito
Birnam Wood Golf Club – Montecito
Glen Annie Golf Club – Goleta
Rancho San Marcos Golf Course – Santa Ynez Valley (off Hwy 154)
Alisal Golf Course – Solvang
River Course at Alisal – Solvang
La Purisima Golf Course – Lompoc
Marshallia Ranch Golf Course – Lompoc
Village Country Club – Lompoc
Rancho Maria Golf Club – Orcutt
Sunset Ridge Golf Center – Santa Maria
Monarch Dunes Golf Club – Santa Maria

TIP
Twin Lakes is a great place for beginners and offers an early bird special, 7-9 a.m., $8 for 9 holes. Looking for a challenge? Check out La Purisima. Go ahead . . . take a mulligan. I won't tell.

CARVE AND GRIND
AT SKATER'S POINT

If you've got little groms in your house who'd rather surf the streets than walk down them, head on over to Skater's Point, Santa Barbara's oceanside skate pond. Grind your board against the concrete edges and carve inside the sculpted twelve thousand-square-foot arena while taking in the epic views of the beach and Stearns Wharf.

If you're looking to upgrade your board or want to add to your collection of sweet rides, head on over to the wood-walled board shop, Arbor. They have a unique display of eco-friendly rides for both skaters and snowboarders that are made with high-end woods like walnut and bamboo. And be sure to browse the selection of sunglasses and outerwear, too. It's pretty sick, bruh.

Skater's Point, Cabrillo Blvd. and Garden St., Santa Barbara
sbparksandrecreation.com

Arbor Santa Barbara, 14 W Anapamu St., Santa Barbara
arborcollective.com

Neighborhood: Downtown Santa Barbara
Kid friendly

PAINT A MASTERPIECE
AT THE PAINTED CABERNET

Ever wondered how anyone could create a painting and make it look so easy? Well, get ready to paint some happy little trees and other things while sipping wine at The Painted Cabernet. Go to the website to choose the night you want to attend and the painting you want to learn how to make. Then show up ready for super-casual painting instruction and a good time while the teacher leads you step-by-step through a fun, laid-back class. Bonus: All the materials are provided with the cost of the class, plus a complimentary glass of local wine, beer, or champagne.

Each class lasts about two hours and is kicked off with lively music. They make for great date nights or mixing up girls' night out. And when the class is over, don't forget to take your masterpiece home with you so you can ooh and aah over your own work of art for years to come.

The Painted Cabernet, 1229 State St., Santa Barbara, paintedcabernet.com

Neighborhood: Downtown Santa Barbara
Not kid friendly

TIP
Book early as their classes tend to sell out quickly! And if you want to book a private group party or an off-site event, they have a Van Go (heh!) to meet your needs.

DO YOGA
ON THE BEACH

Sure, you can do yoga inside at any number of yoga studios in town. But why would you stay indoors when it's a constant sunny seventy degrees here and there's a $5 yoga class on the beach?!

Every Sunday at 11 a.m., you can get your stretch on with a stellar view of the ocean at Leadbetter Beach. Don't have a yoga mat? No problem! Your super-casual instructor, Mike, brings all the goods including fun funky music that plays throughout the one-hour class.

If you're new to yoga, don't be intimidated! This community-based yoga class is the perfect spot to try new things while those around you breathe, stretch, and giggle their way through this ultra-casual class.

Transcends Yoga With Mike, 402 E Ortega St., Santa Barbara
transcendsyogawithmike.com

Neighborhood: Downtown Santa Barbara
Kid friendly

TIP
Great place to bring your kids for yoga! It's totally family friendly.

DO A NITE MOVES
AQUATHON

Every Wednesday night, late April-August at Leadbetter Beach, you'll see dozens or hundreds of crazy race fanatics or first-time racers go big or go home at the Nite Moves aquathon race.

Show up at Leadbetter Beach and get ready to race your heart out like a true biathlon god. Suit up in a wetsuit (if you've got one), line up with the group of competitors, and dive into the chilly waters as soon as you hear the whistle blow for a quick half-mile swim around the ocean buoys. Next, strip down and throw on those running shorts like you're used to changing in public, and take off for an easy 5k with a sweet scenic view.

Once you catch your breath, grab your free t-shirt and head for the nearest food stand to get your grub on as you watch the sun set behind the cliffs of the mesa.

Run Santa Barbara , Races start and end at Leadbetter Beach
runsantabarbara.com

Neighborhood: Downtown Santa Barbara
Kid friendly

TIP
Got kiddos who want to get in on the action? They've got kid events listed on their website, too. But a quick note to all you slow-moving surfers, the race starts at 6:35 p.m. sharp, so, don't be late!

CAMP ON THE BEACH

There's nothing sweeter than getting a little fresh air in the great outdoors. And it's an even better experience when your bed is a custom memory sand mattress. If you haven't camped on the beach and had a bonfire at night, you haven't really done the Southern California travel thing yet. Book a night or two at Carpinteria State Beach or Refugio for a California-style camping trip—and don't forget your roasting stick!

Not much of a camper? Get your glamp on at El Capitan Canyon where the safari tents and cabins have plush bedding in the rustic-style sleeping quarters. The best part is the campground is just a stone's throw from El Capitan beach, but not so close that you'll get all that pesky sand everywhere.

Neighborhood: Carpinteria or Refugio
Kid and dog friendly

TAKE A HIKE
AROUND SANTA BARBARA COUNTY

There is no shortage of hiking trails near and far in SB County, but the most notable hikes on the list are Inspiration Point and Manzana Schoolhouse.

If you're looking for a short butt-kicking hike to the top that's popular with the locals, check out Inspiration Point to get a 365-degree view of Santa Barbara and the mountains behind. But if you're looking for an all-day hike with some history behind it, check out Manzana Schoolhouse and Dabney Cabin.

Bring plenty of water and snacks for this seventeen-mile hike to an area that has an abandoned schoolhouse and homes from early settlers of the Santa Ynez Valley. Read up on the hike before heading out so you know what to look for and then follow the detailed directions from the website so you don't get lost!

Santa Barbara Hikes, santabarbarahikes.com

Neighborhood: All over Santa Barbara County
Kid and dog friendly

TIP
Be sure to bring water for yourself and Fido as some of these hikes get a little gnar and can be really strenuous if heat is a factor.

Other notable hikes in Santa Barbara that are a must-do include:

Tangerine Falls
all of the Falls hikes are awesome to do
after a good rainy winter season

Seven Falls

Nouqui Falls

Rattlesnake Trail
excellent bouldering and a relatively short hike
depending on your rock hopping skills

Cold Springs Trail
a classic hike that is suitable for
most novice or experienced hikers

McMenemy Trail
good hiking and running trail with a larger-than-life view of
the ocean and mountains both coming and going

Cathedral Peak
gnarly all-day hike on a primitive trail
shared with Class 3 rock climbers

Neighborhood: All over Santa Barbara County
Kid and dog friendly

GO ROCK CLIMBING
AT LIZARD'S MOUTH

Aside from the well-outfitted Santa Barbara Rock Gym, Lizard's Mouth is arguably one of the best beginner spots for new rock climbers and a haven for Class 3 climbers looking to test their skills in the real world.

Take a drive up Highway 154 and take a left onto Kinevan Road. Stay to the left at the fork in the road, which will put you on West Camino Cielo Road. From there it's pretty much a straight shot to the top of the mountain. Shortly after you pass the big water tank on the right and the metal gate on the left that says "No Shooting," pull over into the orange-y sand turnout spot. You'll probably see other cars there, too.

Look for footsteps in the sand or just go for it on the sandstone path (be prepared to forge ahead until you hear voices or see a large clearing with tons of boulders the size of houses). Once you find the spot, make your way up toward the top of the boulders and snake your way around the largest point that sticks up. The underneath side of the mountain/boulder looks exactly like the inside of a lizard's mouth and is an ideal spot for rock climbing.

The directions and the trailhead may be a little vague, but if the drunk high school kids can find it every year so can you.

Santa Barbara Hikes, santabarbarahikes.com

Neighborhood: Between Santa Barbara and Santa Ynez Valley
Kid and dog friendly

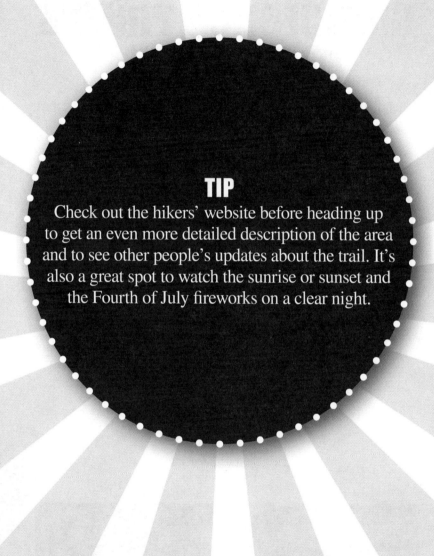

TIP

Check out the hikers' website before heading up to get an even more detailed description of the area and to see other people's updates about the trail. It's also a great spot to watch the sunrise or sunset and the Fourth of July fireworks on a clear night.

GO BLUEBERRY PICKING
AT RESTORATION OAKS

Pretend like you're Laura Ingalls Wilder of *Little House on the Prairie* and pick your own blueberries at Restoration Oaks.

Slow down for an afternoon and take a leisurely drive out to Restoration Oaks in Gaviota, off Highway 101, for a true country-style experience. Roll up to the wood shack, grab a bucket, and get to pickin' while black-tailed deer saunter around the property and red-tailed hawks soar overhead. In about fifteen minutes you can easily pick about 2.5 pounds of blueberries!

When you're finished, head back to the shack and get your berries weighed by the pound before you pay and go home to your fruity feast.

Seasonal activity every June and July.
Depending on the weather, April-August.

Restoration Oaks, 402 E Ortega St., Santa Barbara
santabarbarablueberries.com

Neighborhood: Gaviota
Kid friendly

TIP
Call ahead before making the trek out there to be sure the berries are in season.

· ·

GO FREE DIVING
AND SPEAR FISHING

Act like a native and try your hand at spear fishing in some of the choicest waters in Southern California. Go to Blue Water Hunter in the Santa Barbara Harbor, ask for Andy, and let him guide you through the store. Then schedule a dive trip with the crew and, if possible, reserve a spot on a trip to San Clemente, the southernmost island of the Channel Islands that the locals call the Garden of Eden.

If you really want to get the inside scoop on what's what, join the Santa Barbara Freediving Club where you don't have to be a member to get a sweet rate on a dive trip. Find them on Facebook to get all the details and meet up with the crew every first Thursday of the month.

Check out Mesa Lane near Thousand Steps for lobster during the fall, Refugio Cove any given weekend for a wide variety of fish, or Gaviota Beach during halibut season.

Blue Water Hunter, 117-D Harbor Way, Santa Barbara, blueh20.com

Neighborhood: Santa Barbara Harbor
Not kid friendly

TIP
Save a few bucks and get a 4/3 wetsuit since it's a good crossover sport suit that you can use for snorkeling or surfing.

SNORKEL
AT MESA LANE

Hands down the best snorkeling in SB: Mesa Lane.

Walk down Thousand Steps (the entrance is on Santa Cruz Boulevard which is actually a short dead end street) and plunge into the chilly waters dubbed Mesa Lane. On a high visibility day in summer or late fall you're likely to see bat rays, baby leopard sharks, guitarfish, rockfish, garibaldi, calico bass, perch, and spider crabs. In need of some snorkel gear? Check out Santa Barbara Aquatics in Old Town Goleta (a.k.a. north end of Hollister Ave).

Thousand Steps, Santa Cruz Blvd., Santa Barbara

Santa Barbara Aquatics, 5822 Hollister Ave., Goleta

Neighborhood: Santa Barbara Mesa
Kid friendly

TIP
Check yourself before you wreck your . . . swim. Check windalert.com and Google the NOAA swell report for SB before going out. Large swell and windy days can make for a bummer swim.

TAKE
A SCUBA LESSON

Just about anything water sport-related can be found at SEA Landing in the harbor. So, if you're looking to take a scuba lesson or trip, get on board the Truth Aquatics boat and set sail for the Channel Islands where you'll see a myriad of fish and underwater novelties.

Are you already an experienced diver looking for the good spots? Check out Refugio for shore dives or Gaviota . . . although it can be a little wishy-washy some days. Your best bet is going to be the islands, specifically Santa Barbara Island and Cortez Bank where there's an ocean ridge full of lobster.

Truth Aquatics, 301 W Cabrillo Blvd., Santa Barbara, truthaquatics.com

Neighborhood: Santa Barbara Harbor
Not so kid friendly

TIP
UCSB students, you can take an intro course through the school and the cost/trips are way cheaper.

GO
DEEP SEA FISHING

Head on over to SEA Landing and charter a trip with Stardust Sportfishing for a three-quarter-day island trip or half-day coastal fishing trip. You'll find white sea bass and halibut on a three-quarter-day trip to Santa Cruz or Santa Rosa Islands. Is rockfish more your flavor? Do a half-day trip that lasts about six hours and keep your fingers crossed that the fish will be biting!

Wanna save a few bucks and fish from land? Check out Goleta Pier where you can fish from the boardwalk without a license. Just keep your feet on the pier as shoreline fishing requires a license and the fish and game wardens are always around.

Get some good gear before you head out at Hook, Line, and Sinker on Calle Real near Highway 154 and say hello to the owner, Cap'n Bacon. And keep an ear out for the mackerel run that happens late spring/early summer where you can bring in pounds and pounds of fresh fish!

Stardust Sportfishing, 301 W Cabrillo Blvd., Santa Barbara
stardustsportfishing.com

Hook, Line, and Sinker, 4010 Calle Real, Santa Barbara
hooklineandshooter.com

Neighborhood: Santa Barbara Harbor and Goleta
Kid friendly

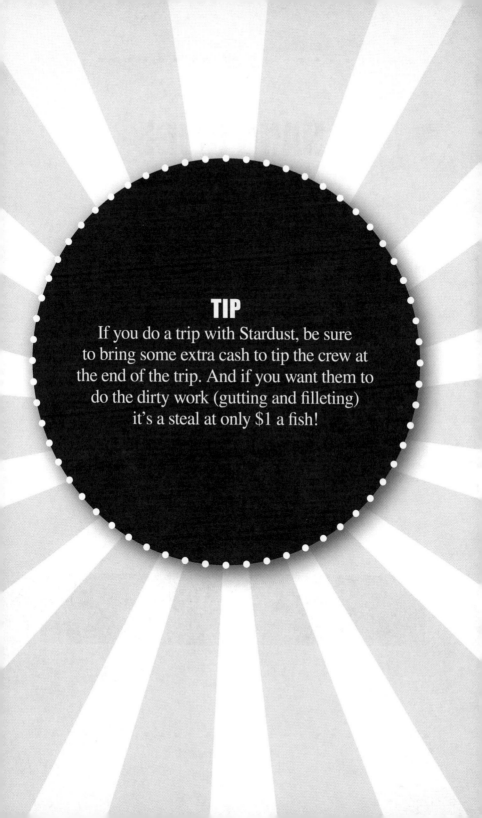

TIP

If you do a trip with Stardust, be sure to bring some extra cash to tip the crew at the end of the trip. And if you want them to do the dirty work (gutting and filleting) it's a steal at only $1 a fish!

HANG GLIDE
IN ELINGS PARK

Ever had that dream as a kid that you could fly with the birds? Me, too. And now is your chance!

Sign up for a one-time "just for funsies" soaring adventure or get serious with some lessons at Fly Away Hang Gliding. Once you sign up for an outing, meet Willy, your friendly instructor, on one of the best training hills in the country on the south side of Elings Park. After some training info of dos and don'ts get ready to soar above it all any day of the year (weather permitting). And if you decide to get serious about the sport, it's easy-peasy to switch into go mode as the lessons cost the same as a fun novelty outing.

Fly Away Hang Gliding, flyawayhanggliding.com

Neighborhood: Santa Barbara Mesa
Kid friendly

TIP
There's no minimum age for going tandem. So, go ahead! Make some memories with your kiddos.

TAKE TO THE SKIES
IN A GLIDER PLANE

If you were born before the '90s and ever played with an Atari joystick then you're ready to go for a ride in a glider plane. Take to the skies with Santa Barbara Soaring, a husband-and-wife team-company that takes you on personal trips in their glider planes. Go on a solo mission or bring a buddy and let your pilot take you on quick fifteen-minute runs or longer two-hour rides that showcase famous ranches and properties in the valley and Santa Barbara.

Wanna fly it? You can do that, too! These guys offer everything from short rides to full pilot license training. So, put your aviators on and get ready to steer your silent flight with the stick like an ace, Maverick.

Santa Barbara Soaring, 900 Airport Rd., Santa Ynez
sbsoaring.com

Neighborhood: Santa Ynez
Kid friendly

GO SAILING
WITH A PRO

If you don't have a friend with a sailboat, you can still get your sea legs and learn a few things with Santa Barbara Sailing. Take to the sea for a couple hours with a small group of four people as you sail the low seas on a twenty-two-foot Capri or J24 around the Santa Barbara Harbor for less than $100. If you want to take it to the next level and go pro, leave the eye patch at home and sign up for their certification program.

Santa Barbara Sailing, sbsailing.com

Neighborhood: Santa Barbara Harbor
Kid friendly

RUN A RACE

There's a race to be run just about every month in Santa Barbara and there's a wide range of them from really fun ones including costumes or wine tasting to the super challenging. These are the top races that are sure to fill up every year, listed in calendar order:

New Year's Resolution Run – Leadbetter Beach, Santa Barbara

Orchard to Ocean Run – Carpinteria

Mesa Trail Running Series – Elings Park, Santa Barbara

Are You Tough Enough? – Santa Barbara

Santa Barbara Chardonnay 10-Miler & 5k – Leadbetter Beach Santa Barbara

Gaucho Gallop – UCSB, Goleta

State Street Mile – State St., Santa Barbara

Semana Nautica 15k – San Marcos High School, Goleta

Westmonster 5k – Westmont College, Montecito

Pier to Peak Half Marathon – Stearns Wharf, Santa Barbara

Mesa Trail Running Series – Elings Park, Santa Barbara

Carpinteria Kiwanis Big Avocado Run – Carp Bluffs, Carpinteria

Santa Barbara Veterans Day Marathon and Half Marathon – Downtown Santa Barbara

UCSB Turkey Trot – UCSB Lagoon, Goleta

Thanksgiving Day 4-Miler – Magnolia Shopping Center, Goleta

Eling Terrain Festival – Elings Park, Santa Barbara

GO SKYDIVING
IN LOMPOC

Load up on a good breakfast and drive out to the Lompoc Airport for the rush of your life. After you fill out the novel-length waiver and watch a video that will scare you straight into following all the rules, head out to the hangar to receive your manifest. Then get filmed and interviewed by your seasoned instructor before you hop onboard the fastest-climbing single engine skydiving plane in the world. Your film crew (aka the instructor) will follow you onto the plane where you'll make your way up to thirteen thousand or eighteen thousand feet before making your tandem jump.

On the way down, be sure to take in the view and say hello to the camera attached to the instructor's left wrist. After your 120-mile-an-hour plummet back to earth, the chute will open up (you'll stop screaming) and you'll slowly, peacefully drift back to land.

During the summer, as the plane gains altitude, enjoy an ocean view and take in the scenery of Point Conception, Jalama, and the Channel Islands. During the winter, you can see the Guadalupe Dunes where part of *Pirates of the Caribbean: At World's End* was filmed.

Sky Dive Santa Barbara, skydivesantabarbara.com

Neighborhood: Lompoc
Not kid friendly, minimum age is 18.

· ·

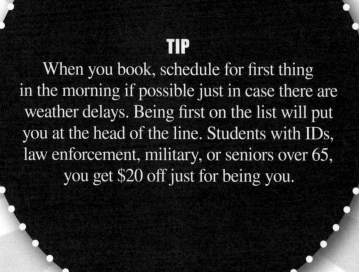

TIP
When you book, schedule for first thing in the morning if possible just in case there are weather delays. Being first on the list will put you at the head of the line. Students with IDs, law enforcement, military, or seniors over 65, you get $20 off just for being you.

GO HORSEBACK RIDING
ON THE BEACH

Horseback rides are always fun, but when you ride on the beach it's downright magical. And for many, it's absolutely romantic and the perfect way to propose to their sweetheart.

Choose between a morning, afternoon, or sunset ninety-minute, guided ride on Summerland's beach or through the back trails that lead to Montecito. Along the way, you'll hear stories about Santa Barbara celebs as your guide points out the homes and properties as you pass by. Each ride is done in groups of six or fewer people. So, you're likely to hear everything your guide is saying along the way and it makes for a nice, semi-private ride. If you've ridden before, you'll have a chance to trot and canter as you take in the beautiful scenery of the beach or surrounding orchards and mountains.

If you've got little guys who are ready to cowboy up, check out the Summer Horse Adventure, led by the seasoned lead guide, Charlie. Every Tuesday and Thursday morning during the summer, kids (ages 5-12) are taught lessons while the little ones are taken on pony rides and taught how to care for the mini horses.

Santa Barbara Beach Horseback Rides, sbbeachrides.com

Neighborhood: Summerland
Kid friendly

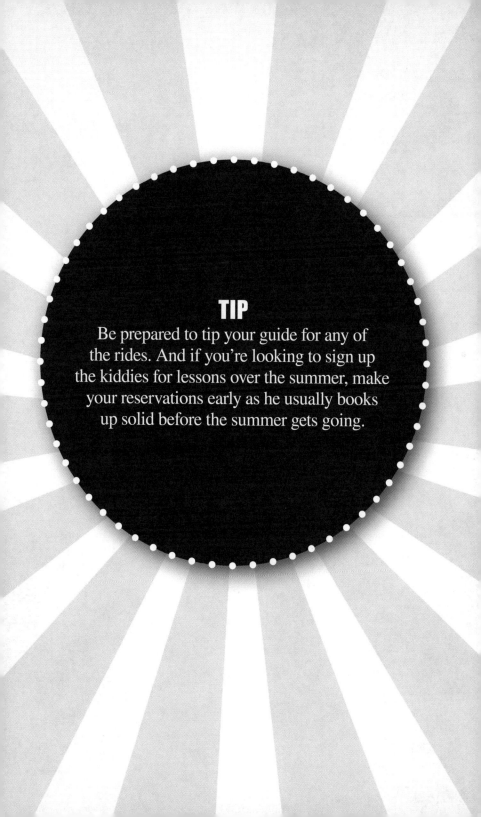

TIP

Be prepared to tip your guide for any of
the rides. And if you're looking to sign up
the kiddies for lessons over the summer, make
your reservations early as he usually books
up solid before the summer gets going.

CULTURE AND HISTORY

TAKE IN A 360-DEGREE VIEW
OF SANTA BARBARA

Looking to get above all the hustle and bustle of the downtown city streets? Take a short hike up the winding staircase at the Santa Barbara Courthouse to the top of the watchtower to get a full 360-degree view of the land and sea. On a clear day you'll get a glimpse of the four Channel Islands, the tops of historic buildings, and the surrounding mountains.

On your walk back to earth, check out the one-hundred-year-old mural on the second floor and then make your way down the spiral staircase covered in Spanish tile on the far side of the building. Lean over the railing to get a glimpse of the Sunken Gardens on the back side of the courthouse filled with an abundance of Santa Barbara's native plant life.

Looking for a tour of the courthouse? You've come to the right place! Free guided tours are offered every Monday, Tuesday, Wednesday, and Friday, 10:30 a.m. and 2 p.m. Don't forget to tip your docent!

Santa Barbara Courthouse, 1100 Anacapa St., Santa Barbara
santabarbaracourthouse.org

Neighborhood: Downtown Santa Barbara
Kid friendly

● ●

PARTY IN THE STREET
DURING OLD SPANISH DAYS FIESTA

There's a party going on and you're invited! For one week in August, Santa Barbara takes a hiatus to celebrate its Spanish and Mexican heritage during Old Fiesta Days.

The streets of the city (and later your car mats) are filled with confetti while residents and out-of-towners alike enjoy watching the largest horse parade in the world clip-clop down State Street, experiencing a Spanish dance show at the Old Mission Santa Barbara, and eating a ton of authentic Mexican food in De la Guerra Plaza.

Buy a few eggshells filled with confetti on State Street and feel free to break them over anyone's head while you make your way to the nearest taco truck and/or margarita stand. It's a free-for-all, take-the-whole-day-off kind of good time that even the mayor of the city enjoys!

On the last day of Fiesta, cruise along with a thousand other bike riders for the decades old tradition of riding from Stearns Wharf to Goleta Beach, complete with boom boxes, sombreros, and every bicycle style imaginable. Olé!

First Week in August

Old Spanish Days Fiesta, www.oldspanishdays-fiesta.org

Neighborhood: Downtown Santa Barbara
Kid friendly

VISIT
THE QUEEN OF THE MISSIONS

Relive your fourth grade California history days by visiting the Queen of the Missions, Old Mission Santa Barbara. With an expansive surrounding rose garden, tended by local volunteers, the Santa Barbara Mission boasts a rich and diverse two-hundred-year history complete with the only burial crypt room in a California Mission. Take note of the panther paw print in the tile work and the horse hoof markings in the redwood ceiling beams.

To get all the details, choose between docent-guided tours of art and architecture or La Huerta Historic Gardens, housed within the Mission walls. If you're looking to run solo through the Mission, do the Basic Tour Route, a self-guided tour of the Sacred Garden, the Historic Cemetery, the Church, and the nine rooms that make up the museum. Wanna hit up all the missions in Santa Barbara County? Check out Old Mission Santa Inés, as well, in Solvang.

Old Mission Santa Barbara, 2201 Laguna St., Santa Barbara
santabarbaramission.org

Old Mission Santa Inés, 1760 Mission Dr., Solvang, missionsantaines.org

Neighborhood: Downtown Santa Barbara
Kid friendly, but geared toward fourth grade and older.

TIP

To get in on a docent-guided tour, be sure to make your reservations at least two weeks in advance.

BECOME A SANTA BARBARA
HISTORY BUFF

Brush up on your California history by taking a casual stroll or a guided tour through the oldest neighborhood and adobe buildings in town, all within a four-block radius. Get an up-close look at the Spanish relics that first graced Santa Barbara's shores, wander through the Cañedo Adobe, and learn about the second oldest building in California, El Cuartel, that once housed two soldiers' families during the founding of our fair city.

Take a gander across the street from El Presidio to see Santa Barbara's first Chinatown. Then let your imagination run wild as you hear stories about the larger-than-life fiestas thrown by José de la Guerra, the fifth comandante of the Spanish army who once resided in Casa de la Guerra.

El Presidio de Santa Bárbara State Historic Park
123 E Canon Perdido St., Santa Barbara, santabarbaracourthouse.org

Casa de la Guerra, 15 E De la Guerra St., Santa Barbara, sbthp.org/casa

Neighborhood: Downtown Santa Barbara
Kid friendly, but geared toward 4th grade and older.

TIP

Buy admission to El Presidio de Santa Bárbara State Historic Park to get free admission to Casa de la Guerra. And take a break from the history lesson for a quick bite at Three Pickle's Deli inside old Chinatown's first building across the street from El Presidio.

DO THE 1ST THURSDAY ART WALK
IN SANTA BARBARA

Walk around downtown for a free night of art and culture while you snake your way through various galleries and stores on State Street and La Arcada. Catch previews of upcoming plays, symphony performances, dance productions, and (of course) up-and-coming artists showcasing their talents. Most of the galleries or museums offer glasses of wine or small bites, which makes for a fun twist on the usual hors d'oeuvres before dinner. It also makes for a great date night!

Every first Thursday of the month, 5:00-8:00 p.m. (rain or shine)

1st Thursday, Located mainly between Victoria and Cota Sts. in downtown Santa Barbara, downtownsb.org

Neighborhood: Downtown Santa Barbara
Not super kid friendly

TOUR
LOTUSLAND

Montecito, where the one percent live, is full of estates and wealthy homes, most of them behind large gates that only Spiderman could scale. Ganna Walska Lotusland, however, is open to the public for guided tours and is one of the most awe-inspiring properties. Discover the estate's multiple gardens such as the rainforest garden or the rarest and largest collection of cacti from around the world.

And like most Montecito estates, Lotusland has a fascinating history and the tour guides tell a wild Real Housewives-type story of its previous socialite owner, Ganna Walska.

Ganna Walska Lotusland, lotusland.org

Neighborhood: Montecito
Kid friendly depending on age and attention span.

TIP
Lotusland is by reservation only.

GO TO THE
I MADONNARI FESTIVAL

Once a year local art supplies are splayed all over the parking lot in front of Old Mission Santa Barbara while artists get to work on their 12 x 12 foot spaces creating art with pastels that lasts for several weeks. Sponsored by local businesses, the 150 squares are filled with vibrant works of chalk art by local artists and school kids.

The first day of the festival watch the artists in action and wander in between the taped-off squares while the detailed and ornate drawings are created. Come back the next day and take a slow walk through the space to see all the finished pieces and enjoy a few bites in the food tents that surround the lot. If you missed the big hoopla weekend, don't stress. The art is on display for several days and even weeks, so long as the weather and foot traffic comply.

I Madonnari Festival, Laguna and Los Olivos Streets, Santa Barbara
www.imadonnarifestival.com

Neighborhood: Downtown Santa Barbara near the Mission
Kid friendly, but leave Fido at home.

TIP
If you've got a budding artist on your hands who would rather be drawing than looking, purchase a square in the children's section for a nominal fee and watch your little artist go!

TALK SHOP
AT CARS AND COFFEE

Set against the backdrop of lux shopping and fine dining, you can ogle and fawn over the hottest rides in town during Cars and Coffee. Stop off at Jeannine's Bakery or Pierre Lafond Market for a cup a joe and a pastry before talking shop with the owners and other enthusiasts as you take a stroll down the street and admire the fine machinery.

Owners of classic cars, hotrods, sports cars, muscle cars, and just about any other type of oldie but goodie on wheels can be found on Coast Village Road every last Sunday of the month or in the Upper Village of Montecito every other Sunday morning 8-10 a.m.

Santa Barbara Cars and Coffee, 1100 block of Coast Village Rd.
Last Sunday of the month
San Ysidro and E Valley Rd. – all other Sundays
sbcarscoffee.com

Neighborhood: Montecito
Kid and dog friendly as long you keep them on a short leash.

TAKE A WALKING TOUR
OF SANTA BARBARA

Downtown Santa Barbara is where the city originally started and has a tremendous amount of history that even the longest-standing local might not know about.

You can take the Red Tile Tour, a self-guided tour via podcast and map, for free. Listen to Seinfeld's J. Peterman (John O'Hurley) tell you tidbits and highlights of local history as you walk all over the downtown area soaking up the architecture and sunshine.

For a more in-depth historical tour, join one of the weekend architecture tours, Sabado or Domingo, hosted by the Architectural Foundation of Santa Barbara. Show up at the appointed location and keep an eye out for your guide, a local architect. (They're usually carrying a binder and look somewhat official.) You'll be guided through the city on these walking tours and told the history of various building structures and the historical events that took place on each block. Just a heads up: It's a suggested donation tour that funds the architecture scholarship foundation.

Red Tile Tour, "Google Beyond the Rooftops podcast by John O'Hurley"
Architectural Foundation of Santa Barbara, afsb.org

Neighborhood: Downtown Santa Barbara
Kid friendly, if your kid is a history enthusiast.

TIP

Find a good parking spot as the architecture tours usually run overtime. And be sure to wear comfortable walking shoes. You'll end up walking farther than you thought!

DO THE ART WALK
ON CABRILLO BOULEVARD

Every Sunday, 10 a.m. till dusk, Santa Barbara's most picturesque street is covered in arts and crafts the likes of which you'll not see at your average county fair or flea market. Walk down the palm tree-lined street on the ocean side, and wander through the dozens of freestanding art booths and display tables.

Many of the artists are regulars who are on the street each week, while others come and go. But the best part about checking in on the arts and crafts show every once in a while is getting first dibs on an up-and-coming artist's or jewelry maker's first piece. Bring cash and get ready to spy unique goods like hand-blown glass jewelry or landscape paintings.

Santa Barbara Arts and Crafts Show, East Cabrillo Blvd. at State St.
Santa Barbara

Neighborhood: Downtown Santa Barbara
Kid and dog friendly

TIP
If your kiddo is prone to wandering off, maybe get a sitter as Cabrillo Blvd. is one of the busiest traffic streets in town even though the speed limit is only twenty-five mph.

SEE
SATURN'S RINGS

Once the sun goes down, nerd out with the Santa Barbara Astronomical Unit to see the rings of Saturn as well as other planets, moons, and stars.

Choose the location nearest you (they meet at various places all over the county just about every week) and talk shop like a true science geek as you peer through giant telescopes while the volunteers and fellow astronomy enthusiasts tell you all about the current happenings in the night sky. Be sure to check out the live feed of the moon's surface on one of the members' laptops and ask all those burning scientific questions. Or heck, take your own telescope out for a spin!

Santa Barbara Astronomical Unit, sbau.org

Neighborhood: All over SB County
Kid friendly

SPEND A DAY
IN SOLVANG

Spend a day in the Danish village that looks eerily like the backlot of Duloc from Shrek, starting with a waffle breakfast at Paula's Pancake House. Do lunch at Bacon & Brine for a locally sourced organic pork bahn mi sandwich with a bacon caramel latte served up by Chef Pink. Then take a slight detour and drive a couple minutes down the road toward Buellton to feed the ostriches at OstrichLand USA. Because how often do you get to feed wild-eyed, long-necked birds?

Head back into the village for a nice dinner at Root 246 for a farm-to-table experience. Then top off the night with some sweets at Rocky Mountain Chocolate Factory, like caramel apples or oversized pieces of fudge before heading down the street to the Solvang Festival Theater. Enjoy a night of live theater under the starry night sky in the smallish, seven-hundred-seat theater for a night of culture and country-style refinement.

Neighborhood: Solvang
Kid friendly

TIP
The city parking lot on Alisal, between the windmill and post office, offers free parking all day long.

VISIT
THE REAGAN RANCH CENTER

Not only do we have famous people in this city, we've got former presidents, too! Located near the train station in downtown Santa Barbara, you can visit the Reagan Ranch Center to learn about President Reagan's personal life and ranch home located in the Santa Ynez Valley.

No tickets are necessary to see this historical gem. Just wander inside the center where you'll be greeted by one of the friendly docents who will show you from room to room and regale you with interesting facts about the former president's life outside of the White House. Before heading up the stairs be sure to take note of the guestbook signed by Queen Elizabeth as well as the enormous piece of the Berlin wall. If you can't get enough presidential history, be sure to check out the Reagan Library in Simi Valley.

Reagan Ranch Center, 217 State St., Santa Barbara, yaf.org

Neighborhood: Downtown Santa Barbara
Kid friendly

SPEND A DAY
IN LOS OLIVOS

Don't overlook this one-horse town! Spend the day eating and drinking your way through this quaint country area.

Take a stroll on Grand Avenue, the main drag in town, and go to Los Olivos Café for a French toast soufflé breakfast. If you're more of a skip-breakfast person, grab a cup a joe at Corner House Coffee. Next wander down Alamo Pintado Avenue, the only major cross street, to J. Woeste for a relaxing visit to the country-style succulent garden. After that, head next door to Zinke Wine Co. for wine tasting and a game of bocce ball on their outdoor court.

Grab a quick tri-tip BBQ lunch at R-Country Market and walk around the corner to Pumacasu's where the owners will regale you with folklore stories and make custom jewelry pieces while you continue your wine tasting adventure. Then go next door to Artiste Winery. When you walk in the door, grab the artsy guest book on the left, draw anything you want and sign your name underneath. Stay for a tasting of wines from multiple California vineyards and sidle up to an easel for a chance to create a priceless work of art that could be hung on the ceiling.

Then round out your wine tasting experience with a stop at Saarloos & Sons. When you walk in the door, make a right and head to the original Enjoy Cupcakes counter and order a flight of six mini cupcakes to go with your wine tasting flight. Rather get a chocolate fix instead? Pay a visit to Stafford's Famous Chocolates, a tiny shop located inside the old water tower. When you're ready for dinner, head on over to Mattei's Tavern where the bartender will make you a cocktail based on your mood and the chef will prepare a delectable, locally sourced dinner feast.

Neighborhood: Los Olivos

Most wine tasting rooms are dog friendly, but you should call ahead to the restaurants to see if they have outdoor seating that accommodates Fido.

PET A SWELL SHARK
AT THE SEA CENTER

Ever wanted to swim with the sharks? Well, you can't do that at the Sea Center, but you can pet one! And you can pet a bat ray, sea cucumber, anemone, and starfish, too.

Drive onto Stearns Wharf, one of the last drivable piers in the U.S., and park on the boardwalk. Then walk over to the Sea Center that hangs out on its own section of the wharf where you'll see a collection of sea life up close, pet sea creatures, and even get a chance to dig through the ocean floor. After you're done playing with the fish, head upstairs to view the various species of jellyfish in their ballet-like movements. On your way back down be sure to let the kiddies stop at the marine puppet stage to put on their own show.

Santa Barbara Museum of Natural History Sea Center, 211 Stearns Wharf
Santa Barbara, sbnature.org

Neighborhood: Downtown Santa Barbara
Kid friendly

TOUR
A MONTECITO ESTATE

It's no secret that some of the biggest Hollywood stars—like Oprah and Tom Hanks—own the largest estates and homes in Montecito, but rarely do you get to see the houses and take a tour. Casa del Herrero is your chance to do just that.

When you roll up to the eleven-acre estate you may not be completely wowed by the size of the house, but looky-loos and history buffs alike will be blown away by the architecture, craftsmanship in the details, and the stories behind each piece of décor. After three years and four hundred letters between the owner and the architect, who designed a good portion of downtown Santa Barbara, Casa del Herrero is one of the oldest homes that's still in functional use and boasts extremely detailed metal furniture made by the original owner and rare religious relics from the fourteenth century.

Casa Del Herrero, 1387 E Valley Rd., Santa Barbara, casadelherrero.com

Neighborhood: Montecito
Kid friendly

TIP
Tours are by reservation only. Not just anyone can show up and wander through an estate, you know. But don't let that stop you from going! I heard that Christmastime is the best time to tour the estate as it is fully decorated just as it would have been in the 1920s.

GO
TO A HISTORY MUSEUM

The West Coast may not be the oldest part of the state, but darn it, we've got a whole mess of history! From surf culture to the carriages that brought our ancestors from abroad, SB is bursting with museums on every historical topic you can imagine.

- **Surf Museum** – (Free) Open for just a few hours on the weekends, this funky little museum has been in operation for decades and houses some of the oldest relics of Hawaiian and Californian surf culture.

- **Santa Barbara Museum of Natural History** – By far, one of the best museums in town for the kiddies! Be sure to check out the Curiosity Lab where everything on display is a hands-on experience.

- **Santa Barbara Historical Museum** – (Free) Every few months a new exhibit is brought up from the ten-thousand-square-foot underground vault and put on display for the public. Arguably the best Santa Barbara history museum!

- **Karpeles Manuscript Library** – (Free) Get an eyeful of rare pieces of history like the original Olympic torch and Einstein's famous formula.

- **South Coast Railroad Museum** – (Free) Visit Goleta's train depot built in 1901 and see rooms full of model trains. Afterwards, take the kiddies on a half-mile train ride around the surrounding property and go for a free ride on a handcar every third Saturday of the month.

- **Susan Quinlan Doll & Teddy Bear Museum & Library** – Learn about the history of California through the world of dolls and teddy bears dating back to the late 1700s.

- **Santa Barbara Maritime Museum** – Learn about Santa Barbara's history as a sea-faring town and see unique pieces from historic lighthouses and naval ships.

● ●

WALK THROUGH
TRINITY EPISCOPAL

This one-hundred-year-old mini cathedral is right smack in the middle of downtown and is a sight to see. If you've ever been to Europe then you've seen a cathedral or two. And isn't it always fun to relive a good vacation?

Step inside the entrance to Trinity Episcopal and take note of all the historical plaques on the wall before switching your cell phone to silent and walking into the main sanctuary area. The high-ceiling, sandstone-pillared building with floor-to-ceiling stained glass windows looks exactly like a small French cathedral and was actually designed to mimic the old style. If you wander outside the building, you can take a walk through the prayer labyrinth that is an exact replica of the labyrinth at the Notre Dame in France.

1500 State St., Santa Barbara, trinitysb.org

Neighborhood: Downtown Santa Barbara
Kid friendly

GO
TO AN ART MUSEUM OR GALLERY

Not everyone who lives here is a surfer or beach bum! Santa Barbara has long been known for its artists and diverse cultures. Whether you're looking for a day at the museums or out to discover the next great artist, this eclectic mix of museums and galleries is sure to satisfy your critical eye:

- **Santa Barbara Musum of Art** – Visit Santa Barbara's ultimate in art museums. Collections of pottery, painted works, photography, and installation art can be seen seven days a week. Come on a 1st Thursday Art Walk night and get in for free.

- **Museum of Contemporary Art** – (Free) Located on the top of Paseo Nuevo, this smallish museum of contemporary, installation, and eclectic art is worth a visit. Sometimes there are even interactive art pieces where the public can contribute to an on-going project or piece.

- **Art, Design, & Architecture Museum** – (Free) Visit this on-campus museum located at UCSB where an assortment of collections can be viewed five days a week. Note: The museum is usually closed during the summer.

- **Carriage & Western Art Museum** – (Free) This is the largest carriage museum west of the Mississippi, including Western art, tack pieces, and celebrity saddle collection.

- **Westmont Ridley-Tree Museum of Art** – (Free) Don't overlook this tiny museum, located deep within the Westmont College campus that has exhibited rare and fascinating art pieces from all over the world including pieces created by alumni. Note: The museum is usually closed during the summer.

- **Gone Gallery** – (Free) Go off the beaten path and into the heart of the Funk Zone for a look at some wild-eyed graffiti art. On the walk over keep an eye out for hidden art pieces on the telephone poles that mark the way.

- **Sullivan Goss** – (Free) A fantastic collection of American art that spans 1850-1950 with the occasional current time period art pieces and sculptures.

- **The Arts Fund** – (Free) Discover local artists of all ages and styles. This eclectic mix of art is ever-changing and a great place to start out as an artist or begin your repertoire as a collector.

- **Wall Space Gallery** – (Free) Excellent collection of photography and painted fine art.

- **Santa Barbara Art Glass Blowing Studio** – Visit this unique art store and watch the master in action any day of the week as Saul, the artist, creates his pieces on-site. You can also book a glassblowing class for you and some friends!

- **3D Studio Gallery** – (Free) Super-unique collection of 3D modern art depicting various cityscapes and famous people or events.

SPEND A WEEKEND
IN LOS ALAMOS

If you haven't been to Los Alamos, or "Little LA" as everyone calls it, then you may have blinked and missed it. This one-exit, one-horse town doesn't look like much if you're just passing through, but it's worth a visit toward the end of the week or even a weekend stay.

Everything (and I do mean everything) there is to do in Los Alamos is on Bell Street; the town is the main drag. For a nice lazy weekend, you could definitely spend a whole day and night and see it all without being rushed.

Book a themed room at the Victorian Mansion where you can stay in Paris, Egypt, Rome, or even a pirate suite. Do breakfast at Bob's Well Bread Bakery just a few doors down before heading out for some morning antique shopping at the Gentleman Farmer, a curated boutique store, or the Depot, the town's old train station that takes up nearly a city block. If you're in the mood for a hunt, you've come to the right place. If you head toward the back of the station the prices get a bit cheaper and the hunt gets serious.

For lunch go to Bell Street Farm where they will pack a custom picnic for you, then head for the hills up Centennial Street to the town's county park to enjoy. If you're in a sporting mood, you might even bring a volleyball with you to play on their manmade courts. Otherwise, stay on the main drag and visit Casa Dumetz and Babi's Beer Emporium for some wine and beer tasting for the afternoon.

Do dinner at Union Hotel, the town's old annex to the western saloon-style building in the center of town. Be sure to stop off for a glass of wine first in the saloon where you might catch a glimpse of Kurt Russell sipping his own label, Gogi wines.

Take the San Antonio Blvd. exit, from either direction
on the 101 freeway, and head west onto Bell St.

Neighborhood: Los Alamos
Kid friendly-ish. Leave Fido at home.

VISIT
THE FUNK ZONE

Visit the one area of Santa Barbara that isn't covered in red-tile-roofed buildings, but rather graffiti art and metal siding. The Funk Zone is one of Santa Barbara's oldest neighborhoods of dilapidated warehouses converted to the hippest foodie and artist neighborhood.

Start your exploration with a little wine tasting at the kitschy, hipster-infused Municipal Winemakers tasting room on Anacapa then make your way down wine tasters' row at any number of tasting rooms next door. And if you're visiting on a Sunday, be sure to stop by Corks n' Crowns for a cupcake and champagne pairing with the famous Cupcake Wars winner, Sugar Cat Studio.

Next, make your way into the belly of the beast down the street, as you do lunch or dinner at Lucky Penny, Mony's Tacqueria, or The Lark. Take a little wine tasting break and pop into Guitar Bar, on the corner of Yanonali and Anacapa, for a quick "petting zoo" experience as you ogle the different musical axes hanging from the walls. Then round out your artsy, funky trip with a visit to Gone Gallery on Gray Avenue as you get fully immersed in the small gallery that is covered floor to ceiling in graffiti art.

The Funk Zone, Anacapa, Yanonali, Santa Barbara Sts. below the 101
funkzone.net

Neighborhood: Downtown Santa Barbara

More dog friendly than kid friendly, but kids are always welcome. You might even see a row of dads wearing their babies at the wine or beer bars.

● ●

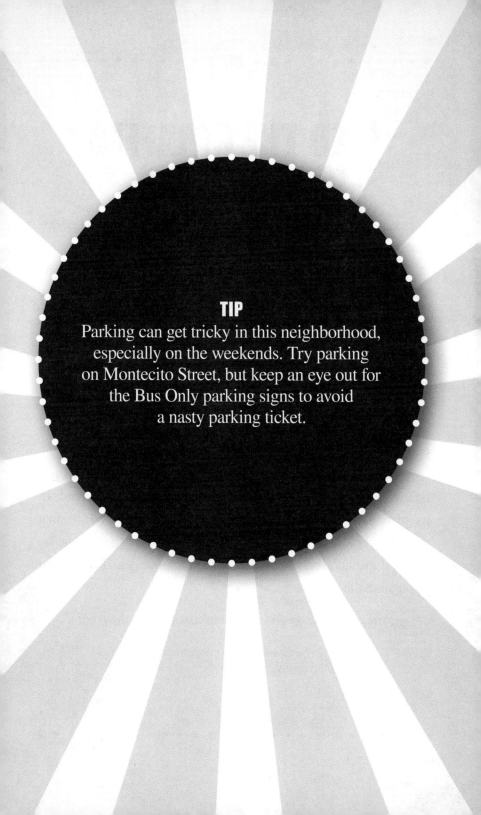

TIP

Parking can get tricky in this neighborhood, especially on the weekends. Try parking on Montecito Street, but keep an eye out for the Bus Only parking signs to avoid a nasty parking ticket.

FEED THE GIRAFFES
AT THE SANTA BARBARA ZOO

Take a walk on the wild side and visit the Santa Barbara Zoo any day of the year (even Christmas Day!).

Bring the kiddies for a romp in the park-like atmosphere with wide sidewalks that make it easy to get around, especially if you have a stroller in tow. Greet the geese on your way into the park and get an up-close look at the flamingos as you wind your way through the hilly area. If you want to get a better look at things, take a free ride on the train and get an insider's take on the different habitats around the zoo. Once you've made your way toward the back, pay an extra six bucks and treat yourself and a giraffe to a little one-on-one time with a personal feeding.

Looking to take your zoo experience to the next level? Buy a backstage pass and meet some of the furry and feathery friends of the place. Or come to the zoo for their annual Zoo Brew beer tasting or Roar & Pour wine tasting events. Be sure to check the website for ongoing special events as things are always buzzing and happening throughout the year.

Santa Barbara Zoo, 500 Niños Dr., Santa Barbara, sbzoo.org

Neighborhood: Santa Barbara
Kid friendly, except for the boozy events.

TIP

If you buy an annual pass you're likely to get your money's worth within the first couple visits. And if you're looking to buy a ticket to Zoo Brew, get your order in the first couple of minutes as tickets usually sell out within ten minutes of their online posting.

TAILGATE
AT A POLO MATCH

You simply haven't lived until you've been to a polo match at the Santa Barbara Polo & Racquet Club. It's like going to a really ritzy church service with champagne, and it's a fabulous place to see and be seen à la Pretty Woman.

Buff the car, put on your Sunday best and a big hat (the bigger, the better!) and enjoy watching immaculately groomed horses and riders gallop up and down the fields for a rousing game of polo. Pack your own picnic and tailgate on the south end of the fields or purchase any level ticket that includes entry or admission to the polo lounge for a decadent buffet experience on the north side. In between matches, take your glass of champagne onto the field for the traditional stomping of the divots and rub elbows with locals and celebs.

May-October, Sundays 1-3 p.m.

Santa Barbara Polo & Racquet Club, 3375 Foothill Rd. #1200, Carpinteria

Neighborhood: Carpinteria
Kid friendly, but you might want to get a sitter if you're planning to really live it up.

TIP
If you're not tailgating, save a few bucks and a minimum twenty-minute wait time in the valet line by parking on the frontage road and walking in.

GO
ON A WILDLIFE CRUISE

Get an up-close, guided view of Santa Barbara County's and surrounding area's wildlife creature habitats with the Wildlife Cruise on Cachuma Lake. The Cachuma Lake Recreation Area offers multiple cruises Friday-Sunday where guests board a boat and learn about the local animals from a park naturalist. You'll see a range of animals from deer to blue heron. And if you're lucky, you'll get to see the bald eagle pair that live nearby and frequently show themselves to onlookers.

If you just can't get enough of the outdoors, make a weekend of it and stay on their spacious campground that overlooks the lake and nearby mountains. And be sure to pop into the Nature Center for a museum-type experience that showcases stuffed local wildlife as well as interactive learning displays about local flora and fauna.

Cachuma Lake Recreation Area, 2225 Hwy. 154, Santa Barbara
sbparks.com

Neighborhood: Santa Barbara near Santa Ynez Valley
Kid friendly

SHOPPING AND FASHION

BUY SOME DESIGNER THREADS
AT JESSICA'S CONSIGNMENT

Versace! Prada! Gucci! Oh my!

Keeping up with the Joneses in Santa Barbara can get a little pricey. So, if you want to walk the walk, but pay a little bit less, head over to Jessica's Consignment for steeply discounted designer threads. Peruse the well-stocked racks of mint condition (probably only worn once or twice) women's clothing, jewelry, and accessories in this small one-room shop while keeping your budget in check. No buyer's remorse here! The only tears you'll be crying when you leave are tears of joy.

Jessica's Consignment, 2008 De La Vina St., Santa Barbara
jessicaconsignment.com

Neighborhood: Santa Barbara's Westside
Leave the kids at home.

SHOP
EL PASEO'S OUTDOOR MALL

Forget those shopping malls you've seen in the movies with gross fluorescent overhead lighting and mall cops on Segways. Paseo Nuevo, located in Santa Barbara's historic El Paseo neighborhood, is California's oldest outdoor shopping mall full of brand names and local eateries in quaint boutique-style shops that could make a monk max out his gold card.

Shop till you drop at hip stores like Kitson for off-the-wall lifestyle and home décor items. Stop by See's Candy for some chocolates where the first candy is free. Then pop into Lush and buy a vegan bath bomb layered with essential oils and flower petals. And when you get a hankering for a bite to eat or a little pick-me-up, stop by Kotuku for fresh juices and mocktails, Hoffmann Brat Haus for German-style brats and Bavarian beers, or Eureka! for gourmet burgers and bourbon tastings.

Paseo Nuevo, 651 Paseo Nuevo, Santa Barbara

Neighborhood: Downtown Santa Barbara
Kid friendly if your kid likes a good old-fashioned shopping
marathon and eating grown-up food.

GET A MASSAGE
IN A SALT CAVE

Take your spa day to the next level—the next level down, that is. Book a massage at Salt, the underground Himalayan salt lounge and cave. Take a walk down the stairs and into what looks like a scene from Aladdin. Ionic salt lamps are plugged in all corners of the dimly lit store and patrons move through the area slowly and quietly before stepping barefoot onto the coarse, salt-laden floors of the pink salt rock-lined meditative caves.

Come for a spa treatment or simply a forty-five-minute meditation session while finely crushed salt penetrates the air to open your airways and refresh your limbic system.

Salt Cave, 740 State St., Santa Barbara, saltcavesb.com

Neighborhood: Downtown Santa Barbara
Not kid friendly

GET A BIKINI
FROM BIKINI FACTORY IN SUMMERLAND

As soon as the weather turns warm in SB (you know, goes from sixty-five to seventy degrees) get yourself over to Bikini Factory for THE best swimsuit you'll ever own.

Feeling a little squeamish about swimsuit season? Don't worry! Bikini Factory has the right suit for any body type or age. This tiny little shack of a shop is packed full of every imaginable style, cut, and color of swimsuit from teeny bikinis to full one-piece swimsuits. And the prices are on par with all the other shops around town.

If all that trying on and taking off works up your appetite, pop next door to Tinker's Burgers, Burgers, Burgers, one of the longest-standing burger shacks in town, before heading to the beach.

Bikini Factory, 2275 Ortega Hill Rd., Summerland, bikinifactory.com

Neighborhood: Summerland
Not quite kid friendly, unless your kid is a girl.

TREAT YOURSELF
TO A SPA DAY AT BACARA

Obviously, there is no shortage of swanky things one could do in Santa Barbara, but if you really want to take your spa experience to the next level a visit to Bacara Resort & Spa is a must.

When you roll up to the resort, swing a left around the gigantic fountain and drop off your car with the handsome valet. Then walk through the grand entrance of this swank hotel as you make your way toward the outdoor walking path and spa area. Once inside the ultra-plush lounge, say yes to the complimentary glass of champagne and let the staff pamper you into a bliss-induced state of mind with a scrub, massage, or rooftop mud bar experience overlooking the ocean.

After your glorious spa treatment, walk your noodle-like legs over to the Spa Café near the spa pool for a leisurely lunch of sashimi on pink Himalayan salt blocks and farm-fresh salad with house-made taro root chips. Not ready to go yet? Lounge by the pool for a few hours or kick back with a cocktail at the bar that overlooks Haskell's Beach.

Bacara Resort & Spa, 8301 Hollister Ave., Goleta, bacararesort.com

Neighborhood: Goleta
Not kid friendly

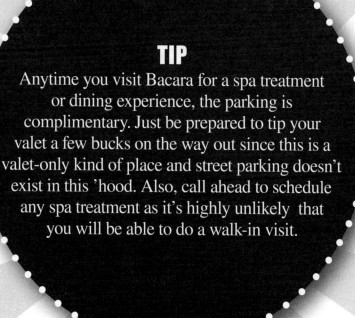

TIP

Anytime you visit Bacara for a spa treatment or dining experience, the parking is complimentary. Just be prepared to tip your valet a few bucks on the way out since this is a valet-only kind of place and street parking doesn't exist in this 'hood. Also, call ahead to schedule any spa treatment as it's highly unlikely that you will be able to do a walk-in visit.

GO ANTIQUING
IN SUMMERLAND

Summerland may be a two-exit town, but it's chock full of nook and cranny antique stores that are sure to have something your home needs.

Start your antique excursion on the town's main drag, Ortega Hill Road, at Just Folk where you'll find an array of curated art pieces alongside collectable Americana décor and antique quilts. Then cross the street to Pine Trade Antiques to search through an excellent collection of gently worn European furniture.

Continue your shopping trip with stops at Summerland Antiques, House 849, and Mary Suding, all within steps of each other on the north side of the road. If you're in the hunting mood, round out your antique search at Antique Collective where they have a huge display of antiques from various dealers.

Neighborhood: Summerland
Not so kid friendly

BUY ONE-OF-A-KIND HOME GOODS
FROM LOCAL MAKERS

The local makers' movement is alive and well in SB and Industry Home and Plum Goods are the showcase floors for all of them. If you're looking for one-of-a-kind pieces to adorn your home and don't mind spending a few extra dollars to keep it local, drop by Industry Home in De La Guerra Plaza for a look-see at the latest digs. Wanna reduce your carbon footprint in a different way? Wander up State Street and get a look at the latest from Plum Goods, a store dedicated to recycled art and eco-friendly digs.

If you're looking for something a little more avant-garde to hang on your walls, stop by Onward on State Street to discover the next great interpretive artist.

Industry Home, 4 E De La Guerra, Santa Barbara, industry-home.com

Plum Goods, 909 State St., Santa Barbara, plumgoodsstore.com

Onward, 1233 State St., Santa Barbara, onwardartanddesign.com

Neighborhood: Downtown Santa Barbara
Kid friendly, if you keep your kid on a tight leash.

BUY SOME VINYL
AT WARBLER RECORDS

Records aren't just for your mom and pop's old turntable anymore. Take a trip back to the good old days with Warbler Records & Goods. This little hole-in-the-wall shop near the Presidio is jam-packed with stacks of vinyl and hipster-style home goods like unique soaps, textiles, and art books. Discover stacks of new and used vinyl records, LPs, and even CDs and cassettes that are sure to rock your music collection.

If you're looking to dust off that old record player and give it a good spit shine, the guys at Warbler also offer repairs and can fix just about any music player you have.

Warbler Records & Goods, 131 E De La Guerra, Santa Barbara
warblerrecords.com

Neighborhood: Downtown Santa Barbara
Kid friendly-ish

STOCK YOUR BAR
AT STILL

If, thanks to Mad Men, you got swept away by the pomp and circumstance of making a good cocktail, or you just enjoy having quality mixers and cocktails at home then stocking up on top shelf goods is a must.

Still, Santa Barbara's only complete barware and mixer store has got what you need. From vintage glasses to rare cocktail shakers to bitters and shrubs, this place can't be beat for finding the best in mixology. The tiny hole-in-the-wall shop is just a hop and a skip off State Street and is chockablock full of anything your home bar could possibly need. So, what are you waiting for, Old Sport? It must be 5 o' clock somewhere.

Still, 37 E Ortega St., Santa Barbara, elevateyourethanol.com

Neighborhood: Downtown Santa Barbara
Not kid friendly

TIP
Not seeing the vintage glasses or barware you want? Come back in a couple months as Jeremy, the owner, restocks the store with new pieces all the time.

GET A PAIR OF COWBOY BOOTS
AT JEDLICKA'S

No need to go all the way to Texas for a pair of cowboy boots, y'all. Jedlicka's in Santa Barbara has a huge store full of the latest styles of western wear including tack room supplies, trendy moccasins, and, of course, cool cowboy boots.

When you enter the store you're ushered in with the sweet smell of leather and hard work. Take a left and wander through the endless racks of shirts and jackets, then make a full loop through the store passing the tack room wares before settling into the forest of boots. Take a seat in the all-leather chairs that look like they've been around longer than the store itself as you try on boot after boot for that perfect Cinderfella fit.

Jedlicka's, 2605 De La Vina, Santa Barbara, jedlickas.com

Neighborhood: Santa Barbara
Kid friendly

TIP
If you're really doing the country thing and don't want to make a trip to the "Big City," swing by their store in Los Olivos, aka The Valley.

BUY AN EXOTIC ORCHID
IN NOLETA

Gardeners, get your gloves on!

The Orchid Estate, located on the border of Goleta and northern end of SB, is an absolute treat to visit for both gardeners and floral appreciators alike. Take a stroll through the various tropical vignettes of exotic orchids that are housed all over the oceanfront property in one of Goleta's hidden suburban neighborhoods. You might even spy a species of orchid you've never seen before as the owners also produce their own hybrids on-site.

If you find something you like, find a friendly groundskeeper to ring you up at the front of the old house. And if you're from out of town, just put in your order as they can ship to any place in the world.

Santa Barbara Orchid Estate, 1250 Orchid Dr., Santa Barbara, sborchid.com

Neighborhood: Noleta (North of SB, not quite Goleta)
Kid friendly

HOST A SPA PARTY
AT FLOAT

A day at the spa is always more fun when you're with your gal pals. Grab six of your closest friends and get over to Float Luxury Spa that is uniquely located in the heart of downtown. What was once a residence from the early nineteenth century has been beautifully redesigned as the cutest little spa in town.

After soaking up the relaxing ambience of low lighting and the cozy fireplace upstairs, head outside to the back patio and lounge near their tranquility pool/fountain. It's oddly quiet for being in the center of town and is exactly as the name suggests. It's luxury, baby.

Float Luxury Spa, 18 E Canon Perdido, Santa Barbara, floatluxuryspa.com

Neighborhood: Downtown Santa Barbara
Not kid friendly

SUGGESTED
ITINERARIES

DATE IDEAS

FUN WITH THE KIDDOS

TREAT YOURSELF

OUTDOOR ADVENTURES

GET CULTURED

INDEX